A NEW LENS ON LIFE

A NEW LENS ON LIFE

JESUS WAS MY OPHTHALMOLOGIST

HARRY R. BRADY

MATER
MEDIA

Published by Mater Media
St. Louis, Missouri
www.matermedia.org

Cover and Interior Design: Trese Gloriod
Editor: Ellen Gable Hrkach

Printed in the USA.

978-0-9913542-4-5

DEDICATION

To all the Sisters of St. Benedict, O.S.B, who instilled in me
the 10 Commandments, especially in memoriam for Sisters
Otillia, Laurentia, and Victoria.

TABLE OF CONTENTS

FIGURES AND PHOTOS

PROLOGUE

A late winter storm had just dropped four to eight inches of snow on the St. Louis region. It had also dropped my enthusiasm for the St. Patrick's Day Parade. My daughter Becky had called me from San Diego and fussed about my shoveling the snow off the driveway. Looking out the window at the snowflakes still falling in the back-yard, I realized that I had made a concession to old age by canceling out on marching in the parade. A few years ago, I would have stubbornly marched without question. What had happened to me? Where was I in my life and how did I get here?

It made me wonder, "why should I have had such a marvelous life, so much fun, so much happiness?" Not everyone has such a wonderful family, an ideal spouse, good friends, good health, professional and financial success.

Is there truly a loving God that comes into your life and provides a way to eternal happiness or is it predes-tined where you fit in the grand scheme of everything? On the other hand, can it be the result of our universe being born by the Big Bang and humanity evolving from some primordial goo, and everyone's existence just the result of this evolutionary process?

Perhaps the answer lies somewhere in between. In any event, I don't know why I have had such a wonderful life. Perhaps by recording my life experiences, someone who reads this can solve the mystery.

1
THE
BEGINNING

The year was 1934. The United States was still in the grip of the Great Depression, and turbulence was everywhere on the planet. Winston Churchill warned the British Parliament of German airpower, and the seeds of WWII were being sown as Hitler and Mussolini met in Venice.

In this country, the FBI had just shot and killed John Dillinger, Public Enemy Number One. Bonnie and Clyde raged through the Midwest in a bloody crime spree. In an attempt to solve the economic woes, President Franklin Delano Roosevelt was authorized by Congress to revalue the dollar.

Amidst all this unrest, citizens looked to movies and sports for escape from reality. Clark Gable received an Academy Award for Best Actor in *It Happened One Night*. The St. Louis Cardinals won the World Series, shutting out Detroit in the final game. Coffee cost twenty-seven cents a pound, round steak was twenty-eight cents a pound, and bread was eight cents a loaf.

Entering the world at this time were individuals whose lives were widely divergent as to personal experiences and philosophies of life. They included the Dionne Quintuplets in Canada, Hank Aaron, Sophia Loren, Ralph Nader, Gloria Steinem, and Harry Brady. The rich and famous don't need to have their story told here, so we will proceed to the obscure.

A son was born on December 26th to Charles Joseph Brady, Jr. and Mildred Dorothy Otillia Estel Brady in their second-story apartment at 618 Lockhart Street, Pittsburgh, Pennsylvania. I was named Harry Robert.

I was the fourth – and last – child in the Brady Family.

Author age 2; author on the left, goat on the right

My father was an automobile salesman struggling to support his family in those tough economic times. My mother was the daughter and eldest child of Christian J Estel and Rose Weber. C.J., as he was called by everyone – including his grandchildren – was a hardworking man who started working at the Armstrong Cork Company at the age of 12, traveling by rowboat to and from work across the Allegheny River. This was the only company he had ever worked for, and he eventually became the plant manager. All the Estels were God-fearing people who made their home at 618 Lockhart Street, across from St. Mary's Catholic Church, a bastion of the fire-and-brimstone German Benedictines.

The house itself was a three-story red brick building that included several additions. It was quite evident that each addition gave no thought to any previous plans or future additions. What is of note is this: in 1857, my great-grandfather, Jacob Estel, a German-speaking brick mason, had worked on the construction of the church. As coincidental as it was, the bricks of the Estel house were identical to the bricks in the church.

The first floor was occupied by C.J., Rosie, and their two unmarried children, Virginia and Robert. Part of the second floor was the Brady residence. There was a kitchen, living room, and one bedroom. The household included my proud parents and my three siblings, Charles J. Brady

III, Mildred Rose, and Virginia Margaret. The remainder of the second floor was a two-room apartment that Aunt Hoo-Hoo (Hilda Rider) lived in with her dog, Snippy. Also on the second floor was an isolated bedroom that my Uncle Bob Estel slept in. The third floor was an unfinished and unheated attic that had two dormers with windows and two unfinished window frames open to the elements. It was family lore that an uncle of C.J.'s had lived up here at one time. The only bathroom for all the residents was strategically located on the second floor opening from a hallway on one side and the Bradys' bedroom on the other. This resulted in rapid bathroom stops for the eleven inhabitants. A side effect of this arrangement was that, if someone forgot to unlock the door opposite the side that they had exited the bathroom, it resulted in some very unhappy people who may have had an urgent need.

The basement had a dirt floor with two small window-like openings to the front sidewalk. The only entry was from a wooden washroom addition to the rear of the kitchen. A trapdoor in the washroom opened to wooden stairs leading down into this foreboding place. To proceed further into the basement, it was necessary to do two things. First, you had to announce your presence to the rat families living there by making loud noises, then listening for them to scurry away. Second, you had to walk down the dark steps to screw in a single bare lightbulb in an overhead socket, the only illumination. It took great bravery for a six-year-old to get something from the basement when my mother asked me to do so.

The front entry from the street was a hallway that ran along the side of the house. There was one door in the hall that opened into a downstairs bedroom. At the end of the hall was another door that opened into a narrow yard. Upon entering the yard, there were three doors from which to choose. One led to Aunt Hoo-Hoo's second-floor apartment. The two other doors led to my grandparents' downstairs apartment. Venturing further into the narrow yard were wooden steps that led up to a porch and the entry into the Bradys' home. Under these wooden steps were the garbage and trash barrels where the rats would play whenever they were chased out of the basement, the washroom, or the downstairs food closet.

Infant mortality was a valid concern in this year. So, the first order of events for a newborn was to have the child baptized into the Holy Catholic Church the first Sunday possible. Since my mother was not able to leave the house on the third day after childbirth, my grandmother and my father took me across the street for this event. Father Lambert, the pastor and a native of Germany, spoke with a very heavy accent. When he was informed that the baby was to be named Harry Robert, he announced that there was no Saint Harry! Therefore, he proceeded to make

Henry Robert Brady a child of God, despite the protestations of those present. One event that I regret not remembering – as I was too young – was my father explaining to my mother that her darling baby, Harry, was indeed a Henry! In any event, my mother, who could cope with anything in life, announced to the world that she "did not give a damn what the priest said. His name is Harry." I hope Saint Peter got the message.

The first memory that I have occurred shortly before my second birthday. Most child psychiatrists claim that first memories occur at an older age. This memory is so vivid that I am certain it happened.

The biggest flood in Pittsburgh occurred during the spring of 1936. My parents took the family to see the Allegheny River overflowing its banks. We got as far as the entrance ramp to the 9th Street Bridge. The river would ordinarily be thirty to forty feet below this level. I remember getting out of the car and immediately becoming frightened as the rapidly-rising river approached the front wheels of our car. Mother picked me up as people were scrambling out of rowboats with their children and pets to get onto the rapidly flooding street. I don't know if we were really in danger, but I do remember feeling safe and secure in my mother's arms.

The second vivid memory occurred at age five. My father had promised to take me (and not any of my siblings) to Minnie's Archery Range to teach me how to use a bow and arrow. My instructions were to wait for him on our front steps, and he would return shortly, then the two of us would go off for a grand time.

I sat and sat and sat and waited and waited. Finally, he turned the corner and came to the doorstep. The excitement was well worth the wait! Dad and I would be going to the archery range together. Without saying a word, he just walked past me and went inside. Surely, he hadn't forgotten that just the two of us were going to Minnie's to shoot a bow and arrow? Nothing was said to me. After a brief time, I went timidly into our apartment and I could hear some loud voices. Moving further into the apartment, my father went into the bedroom and fell into bed. "Mama," I said, "I thought Dad and I were going to Minnie's to shoot with a bow and arrow."

"You can't go today," she said. "Your father has been drinking."

I returned to my place on the front steps alone to ponder why you could not shoot a bow and arrow if you had something to drink.

The front steps became my favorite place to sit to avoid the loud voices and tensions in our home. It also expanded my horizons and allowed me to begin the exploration of the world outside the Brady household and my place in it.

One of my first talents was the ability to identify the

make and model year of any automobile that passed by the observation deck of the front steps. Since there was a stop light at the corner about ten yards from the front steps, it was easy for me to confirm my diagnosis by yelling at the driver, "Hey, Mister, what kind of car is that?"

The commercial value of this ability soon became apparent to my older brother, Chuckie. Six years my senior, he only tolerated his little brother if I did not become too bothersome. Indeed, he was even nice to me when he would win the one- and two-cent bets that the older neighborhood kids would place with him that this five-year-old could correctly identify even the most obscure vehicles. Chuckie's approach to winning taught me that fear has a valid place in performance. An unhappy eleven-year-old got this point across readily to his scrawny little brother.

In retrospect, Chuckie had reason to be so demanding. Being the oldest of four siblings, he was expected by our father to be perfect. No matter what he did, it was not good enough. The way he walked, did his homework, his athletic ability and performance in school were not perfect and were criticized. All of this, regardless of the fact that he was the smartest student in his class and was permitted to skip a grade at Saint Mary's Grade School. This constant demand for perfection may have been a factor in his entering the seminary immediately after graduation from high school. Then he was gone.

BACKGROUND GENEALOGY

Charles Joseph (Red) Brady, Jr. was born July 9, 1902 in Philadelphia, Pennsylvania. He was the son of Irish immigrants Charles Joseph Brady of County Cavan and Margaret V. Kelly born in Londonderry (see genealogy chart).

Red was a child with unlimited potential. A brilliant intellect, his parents sacrificed to send him to a private school run by the Holy Ghost Fathers. Based on his scholastic performance and his athletic prowess, he was awarded a scholarship to Duquesne University in Pittsburgh. He blossomed there playing intercollegiate baseball and hockey, studied the classics, and edited the school magazine. The Holy Ghost Fathers and his mother looked forward to his entering the priesthood. During his collegiate days, two unrelated things occurred that altered that course.

One was meeting and falling in love with Mildred Estel, his first and only love. The other was meeting and having his life controlled by alcohol. Plans for the seminary were discarded. Instead, he obtained a teaching assistant's job at Duquesne and taught the classics.

For her part, Mildred was a popular young lady and had many suitors. Her formal education ended with an 8th grade certificate. She met and fell in love with this dashing college boy and all previous suitors were history. In early 1928, Red and Mildred were married at Saint Mary's, for better or for worse, in sickness and in health, unto death did they part.

Newlyweds Charles and Mildred, 1927

It soon became apparent that a teaching assistant's salary could not support a rapidly growing family. Red drifted into auto sales. It must have been difficult selling cars at the height of the Depression. However, it was impressive to drive up to 618 Lockhart Street in a new model every year.

The family was growing up and Sissy and Jeanie were proving every bit as bright as their older brother. Both girls were permitted to skip a grade at St. Mary's. I remained home for the 1940-41 school year since there was no kindergarten at St. Mary's and it would be anathema to send me to the public school at the end of the block. So, I stayed home and continued to observe life from the front steps.

Then one day, my father disappeared. I knew something was wrong because C.J. was home during the work day and all the adults were in a family conference. I figured it was really important because I was told to go out and play on the front steps. Melting quietly into the background, I heard my grandfather say that he still had some political connections since he had been a delegate to the Democratic National Convention of 1924 (Figure 1.) that had nominated Al Smith to run for president. He promised to go directly to city hall to see if he could get a patronage job for my mother. It was agreed that no one was to discuss the matter any further. At that point, I knew it was best to sneak out to my secure front steps.

Time loses context for children at this age. A year or

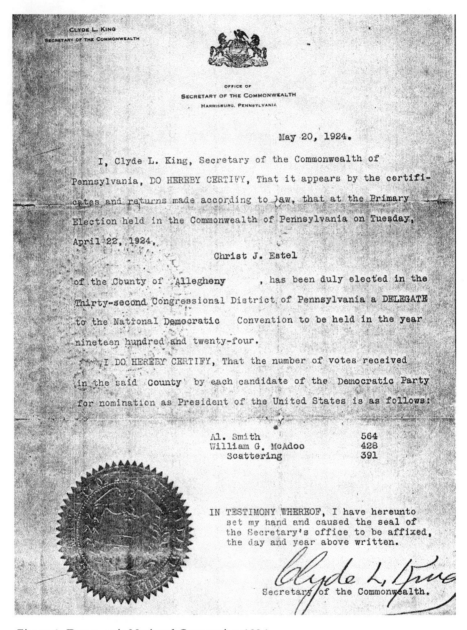

Figure 1. Democratic National Convention 1924

more later, when I was sitting on the front steps, Red came back. He was wearing a dark green jumpsuit and his arms and face were sunburned. Where he was and what had transpired remains unknown to me to this day. The obvious conclusion was that he had been incarcerated somewhere.

Even though my father had reappeared, the family felt that Mildred should keep her steady job since I would be starting grade school and Rosie would be at home when school let out. This changed shortly, when my Aunt Virginia Estel married John Fiedler. The newlyweds needed a place of their own, so they took over the Bradys' apartment on the second floor. The Bradys moved downstairs and C.J. and Rosie moved with Uncle Bob Estel to the suburbs.

In this new arrangement, my mother and dad had their own bedroom, and I shared a second one with my two sisters. The downside of sleeping on the first floor was that I could hear the frightening sounds of the rats gnawing on the floor boards as they were trying to get into the house. They would stop when I stomped on the floor in the vicinity of where they were gnawing. The trick was to fall asleep before they resumed their nightly onslaught. My phobia of rats persists to this day.

Another preschool memory may shed some light on my innovative approach to a wonderful life. At about age five, Tommie T. and I were playing in the sandbox in our backyard. We decided that it would be fun to build a volcano. We built a sand mountain with a large central depression. Why not make it an active erupting volcano? Stuffing the depression with old papers, we soaked them with kerosene that we found in the wash shed and the experiment was ready. Even though we were told not to play with matches, we lit the volcano anyway. What a spectacular eruption! Much more than expected with the flames reaching up to the steps of the wooden porch. Fortunately, my mother was doing the laundry and saw our magnificent volcano as a potential disaster. She and my brother came running out of the house with buckets of water to put a damper on the project.

The Brady Bunch – Virginia, Mildred, Harry and Charles, 1939

Mildred Dorothy Estel Brady

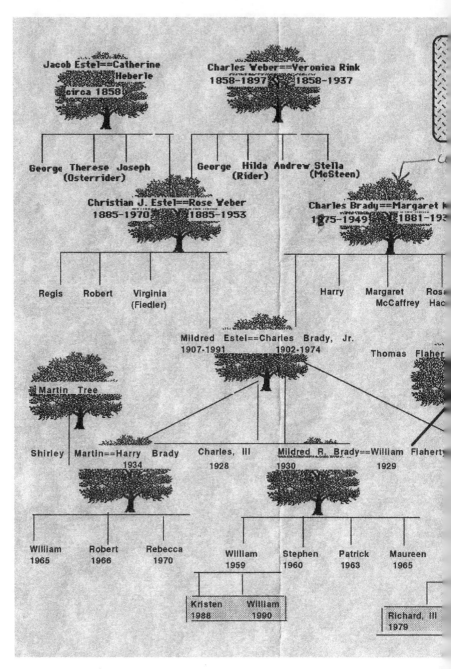

Figure 2. Brady/Estel family tree

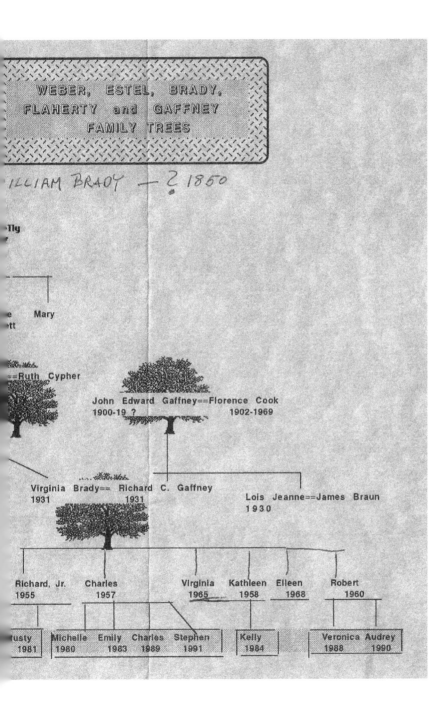

WEBER, ESTEL, BRADY,
FLAHERTY and GAFFNEY
FAMILY TREES

ILLIAM BRADY — ? 1850

lly

Mary
ett

==Ruth Cypher

John Edward Gaffney==Florence Cook
1900-19 ?   1902-1969

Virginia Brady== Richard C. Gaffney
1931   1931

Lois Jeanne==James Braun
1930

Richard, Jr.	Charles	Virginia	Kathleen	Eileen	Robert
1955	1957	1965	1958	1968	1960

tusty	Michelle	Emily	Charles	Stephen	Kelly	Veronica	Audrey
1981	1980	1983	1989	1991	1984	1988	1990

19

2
GRADE
SCHOOL DAYS

First Holy Communion, 1941

Grade school began inauspiciously. With older sisters in the sixth and seventh grades respectively, I was properly escorted to the first-grade classroom. My teacher was Sister Victoria, who appeared to be between 70 and 140. She greeted me and informed my sisters that she was pleased to have another Brady in her classroom since they all did so well and were so well-behaved.

It was evident from day one that the sister's expectations and mine were widely divergent. The first difference of opinion occurred a few days after school had started. Sister Victoria asked me to read something she had written on the blackboard. Try as much as I could, I was unable to see what she had written.

"Oh, come now, your brother and sisters were the best readers in their class."

I looked and strained but could not see the writing.

"Hurry up now. We don't have all day."

I began walking toward the blackboard until I was just a few feet away and began to read the lesson out loud.

"What on earth are you doing?"

Well, what could I do? I read the whole thing as fast as I could so that I could get back to my seat before she could say anything else.

Over the next few weeks, it became apparent that I could not see the blackboard, and my left eye was turning in. Even though we were desperately poor, my mother resolved to take me to the best ophthalmologist in town, Raymond Gray, M.D.

On a Saturday morning, we went to the Jenkins Arcade in downtown Pittsburgh. We found Dr. Gray's office, and after a short wait, we were ushered into a dark room. Dr. Gray asked me to read some letters on a chart. When I could not read them, he did not seem upset. He just kept showing me larger and larger letters until I could read them. Then he put drops in my eyes and left the room for about half an hour.

When he returned, he examined my eyes with several lights. Then he put some strange-looking glasses on me, and I could read all the letters with my right eye, even the tiniest ones. However, my left eye could only read a few of the larger letters. He explained to my mother that I had a lazy left eye and needed glasses for both eyes. In addition, it would be necessary to wear a patch over the right eye to strengthen the lazy left eye. This did not make any sense to me, but my mother said, "You have to do it because this is the best doctor in town." After all, why should you pay for a doctor, then not do what he said?

Well, I was not only the scrawny little kid, but now I was the scrawny little kid with thick glasses and a patch over my right eye. One month later, we went back to the doctor, and just as he predicted, I could read all the letters with either eye! This guy really did know what he was talking about.

Now that my vision problem had been solved, it became time to assert myself academically. When all was said and done, the first-grade primer was not that difficult a book for a child to master, especially if there were three older siblings who learned from the same text. After listening to the same stories being recited by Chuckie, Sissy and Jeanie, it became rote for me. "Alice said come cat, come for dinner. The cat said no, I will find my dinner. The cat went to the barn. The kittens went too. The cat saw a mouse. The kittens saw it too. The mouse ran away." Not too exciting a story. It occurred to me that the only way to liven up this class was to read but hold the book upside down as the sister monitored the performance.

Poor Sister Victoria. She was able to deal with my faulty vision, my lazy eye and an eye patch, but upside-down reading really set her off. The conclusion to this episode was my mother explaining to her and the principal that they just "did not understand Harry." My mother was certainly right on that one.

December 7th, 1941, a "day that will live in infamy," found us at the matinee at the local Garden Movie Theater watching Roy Rogers and his horse, Trigger, beat up the bad guys. In the middle of the movie, it stopped, and an announcement was made that the Japanese had just bombed Pearl Harbor.

From the reaction of the adults in the theater, I knew

this was something bad. Where was Pearl Harbor? On our block or the next street? It didn't take us long in 1941 to hate the Japs. If this sounds racist, please read the accounts of the atrocities the Japanese armies inflicted on prisoners they captured. By the next day, we were shooting Japs in the schoolyard.

A great wave of patriotism soon permeated everyday life. Fathers, brothers, uncles, and neighbors were all joining the armed forces and going to war. My father was too old for the draft and did not enter the service. Uncle Bob Estel was one of the fortunate ones that got drafted and ended up with General George Patton's 14th Armored Division.

He was a radioman in a halftrack, which was a 2.5-ton truck that had tank tracks for rear wheels, a machine gun right behind the driver, and it could follow the tanks wherever they went. His unit helped break through the German lines at Bastogne in the Battle of the Bulge. The newspapers gave a day-by-day account of all the action. The bottom line was that my crabby old Uncle Bob put his life on the line for our freedom.

One afternoon in the second grade, my seatmate (we had double desks) Walter Skryzynski was called to the principal's office. Very shortly thereafter, the principal came and got me from the classroom saying that "Walter needs someone to be with him." We hurried toward her office.

As we approached, I could see Mrs. Skryzynski standing in the hall sobbing. She had just received word that her husband's plane had been shot down on a bombing mission and had crashed into the Black Sea with no survivors. What does a seven- year-old say to one of his best friends who was so proud of his father, a belly gunner in a B-17 bomber? Nothing. I just put my arm around him and we cried together.

By the time I had reached the fourth grade, my sisters had moved on to St. Benedict's Academy, a girls Catholic high school. This left me to carry on the Brady legacy at St. Mary's. Academically it was no problem, but conduct-wise, the sisters still did not understand me. What made matters worse was that my mother could not understand why my grades were straight A's in all subjects, except for a D in conduct.

Perhaps another incident may shed some light on this subject. One particular boring afternoon, the girls took their scheduled lavatory break. The boys were left in the classroom on their good behavior. Since it was a snowy day, all the girls had worn galoshes (boots). Well, red galoshes were the latest style and there were 25 pairs of red galoshes sitting next to each owner's respective desks. What would happen if they were all put in a communal pile in the back of the room? The answer was two hours of total chaos trying to decipher whose galoshes were whose and a total sanity test for one Sister. Even my mother could not understand that one.

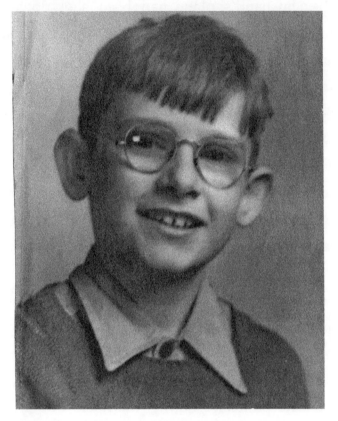

5th grade and the great galoshes extravaganza

The fifth-grade class was assigned a homework project about vocations. I wondered what the quickest way would be to ensure an A plus. I wrote that our pastor and our principal were my role models to emulate. I added a clincher, courtesy of the movie *The Bells of St. Mary's*. I included a picture of Ingrid Bergman and labeled it "Sister Otillia" and a picture of Bing Crosby and labeled it "Father Lambert."

One event occurred on August 6th, 1945, the enormity of which most people did not completely comprehend at the time. On that date, the United States dropped the first nuclear bomb from the Enola Gay, a B-29 bomber, on the Japanese city of Hiroshima. As thousands of Japanese civilians died immediately from the blast and radiation disease became a new scourge for mankind, my only concern was advancing to the sixth grade.

My new seatmate in the sixth grade was Frankie Kello. Frankie was left over from the prior sixth grade class. When I sat down next to the toughest kid in the class, I asked him why he was still in the sixth grade. He informed me that he had flunked, and the sisters said he was dumb. Seizing the opportunity, I told Frankie that he certainly was not dumb, and if he stuck with me, he would never flunk again. That noontime in the schoolyard, I announced to our classmates that if anyone ever called Frankie dumb they would have to deal with me personally.

This seating arrangement became a mutually advantageous association. I taught Frankie the multiplication tables and that a sacrament was an outward sign instituted by Christ to give grace. Frankie taught me how easy it was to steal candy from Murphy's 5 & 10 cent store. Frankie never flunked again, and nobody ever tried to bully the scrawny little kid with glasses.

The sixth grade also brought some of the happiest and

most tranquil times of my childhood. Being selected to be an altar boy was a distinct honor since only a handful of thirty boys were chosen for this honor. "Ad Deum qui laetificat juventutem meam" (to the God who gives joy to my youth) came easily to the younger brother of a seminarian. I think the sisters were still holding out the slim hope for my vocation to the priesthood.

"How angelic can you be?"

Wearing a scarlet cassock and white surplice adorned with a Buster Brown collar and a bright red bow tie was a proud time. Leading the procession at Midnight Mass on Christmas Eve was an experience I will never forget. It was especially neat to see Mary Jane Wasielewski smile at me as the procession passed by her pew. I could tell she was impressed.

By this age, the children were expected to know the Baltimore Catechism by rote. We all knew that we were born "to know, love and serve God in this world, and to be happy with him in the next." Adoration of the Holy Eucharist during "40 hours" provided time for an altar boy to reflect on these topics.

Each altar boy was assigned a thirty-minute period to kneel in front of the open tabernacle. He would then be relieved by the next assigned server. On my first assignment, no one came to relieve me after the first half-hour. Knowing that it would be unthinkable to leave my post, I continued to kneel at the altar. After another half-hour, there was still no relief. This pattern repeated itself five times for a total of two and a half hours! Kneeling there for this length of time was an ample opportunity for an eleven-year-old boy to reflect on the Baltimore Catechism, God, and how this relates to oneself.

Once again, this rekindled the sisters' notion that I might follow my brother into the seminary. What more could I do to convince them that they were sadly mistaken? The opportunity presented itself on the Feast of Epiphany.

There was a heavy snowfall and again, I was to lead the procession into the sanctuary. As usual, the altar boys were involved in some horseplay about five minutes before the sacred ceremony was to begin. Someone pushed me out the back door of the sacristy into a snowdrift and locked the door. Revenge entered my mind and the first person who opened the door was going to pay. Unfortunately, (for him and for me) Father Lambert, our pastor, stuck his head out looking for the leader of the procession, and he got nailed in the forehead with a perfect snowball strike. So, the ceremony began with a very chastised altar boy leading the procession and an unhappy pastor muttering to himself in German bringing up the rear.

Holy Saturday marked the end of the Lenten season and one of the rites was the blessing of the Paschal candle. How could such a solemn event be turned into an utter fiasco? Very easily done by an altar boy and a tub of holy water.

The Paschal candle was very large, ornate and decorated with brightly colored flowers and angels. Father Rabbonus, the assistant pastor, was doing the honors. At a critical point, I was to lower the candle into a large vat of holy water as prayers were being recited. All was going well until it became time to lift this large candle out of the holy water for all the parishioners gathered around the font to see. At this point, the slippery wax surface and gravity took control. The Holy Paschal candle went shooting back into the tub of holy water with a huge splash, blessing all the reverent parishioners.

To salvage as much grace as possible, I grabbed the bobbing candle and pulled it to safety. Unfortunately, the white surplice I was wearing became adorned with bright red, yellow and green splotches. The other altar boy, Larry Kannegeiser, thought this was hilarious and began laughing.

Father Rabbonus, an Austrian immigrant, failed to see the humor and began to berate us in front of the parishioners for turning this sacred event into a farce. Because of his broken English, however, the word he chose for farce sounded like the word for passing intestinal gas. This produced an explosion of laughter from Larry. All I could do was to hold onto the dripping candle for dear life as the good priest kept declaring that we had turned this sacred rite into a fart.

During the Lenten season, Friday afternoons brought the Stations of the Cross. This devout service required frequent genuflections. For reasons beyond me, my sense of decorum was a game I devised called apple bowling. The object of this game was to roll an apple at a girl's leg in the pew in front of you as you genuflected (genuflection puts you in a good bowling stance). Each leg you hit counted as one point. Whoever recovered the apple was next in line to bowl. Sister Laurentia did not see the spiritual benefit of this game.

At this point in grade school, my time outside of class was entirely my own, since both parents were working, and my sisters were busy with high school activities. At noontime, I would heat a can of soup or make a spam sandwich for lunch. After wolfing it down and a brief call to my mother at work, it was back outside. The boys would play softball in the park at the end of the street.

The bell for classes would ring at 12:55 pm and all students were to line up in their assigned places to march into the classroom at 1:00 pm sharp. This obviously led to a confrontation between the ball players and the nuns as the boys would straggle in late. For whatever reasons, I became a representative of the boys to explain this to Sister Otillia, the principal. Despite my best efforts, the sisters were unable to grasp the concept that you can't stop a game in the middle of an inning just because a bell rang. Once again, it necessitated my mother going to the principal's office to explain to the sisters that they "did not understand Harry." One of the factors in my prompt reinstatement to class was that Sister Otillia and my mom had indeed been classmates at this very school. So, after a minute lecture on the virtues of promptness, I would be sent back to class as Tillie and Millie reminisced about their time together at St. Mary's.

No discussion of this period would be complete without speaking about my friend, Albert Tempert. He and his twin sister Alice were classmates throughout grade school. He and I had a common bond since his father was a sheet metal worker who had trouble holding a job. The source of that problem was alcohol.

By this age, I knew what it meant to have too much to drink. Basically, it meant chronic discord and tension in the home when both parents were present. Arguments about sobriety and "drinking up all the money" led the list of controversial topics. So, as soon as school let out, Albert and I were on our own on the streets of the Northside staying away from home as long as we could.

East Ohio Street was the main thoroughfare running through this section of Pittsburgh. It may have been a grand place fifty years earlier, but time, the Depression, and neglect led to a sorry appearance in the 1940's. Added to this was the dreary Pittsburgh climate. Soot, smog, and dirt permeated everything. On overcast days, it was not unusual for automobiles to have the headlights on until noon, due to the dense smog. If it snowed, it would remain white for less than 24 hours before the particulate soot from the steel mills turned everything a dirty gray.

The commercial establishments consisted primarily of pawnshops, saloons, and movie theaters. Albert's older brother, Harold, had a newspaper route and a corner newsstand. Since we needed some spending money and knew it was a venial sin to steal candy and other small items (it would be a mortal sin to steal more than ten dollars or was it $25? The amount varied if you asked the sisters or the priests) we took this opportunity to help Harold by delivering the papers to all the businesses on East Ohio Street. One of the big advantages was the last delivery was to the ticket taker at the Sky Theater. This enabled me to see every Class B movie of this era as he would allow us to sit in the back row as long as we wished.

I already knew most of the bartenders on this route, having been taken to all these places by my father. The usual procedure was for him to have sold a car and come home in a good mood with cash in his pocket. He would be cheerful and pleasant and decide to go out for a walk. I would tag along, and the destination was to Clem Loeffler's saloon, Vinny Loeffler's saloon or to Rheim's café.

We would go in and order a shot and beer for my dad, set up a round for the bar and a soda for me. Then he would settle last week's bar bill with the barkeep. If it had been a particularly good sale, there would be a few nickels for me to play the pinball machine. After the nickels were gone, I would be sent home and he would be follow soon. Soon meant as soon as the cash ran out.

Things would be quiet at home with the children doing their homework. Then peace and serenity would be replaced by chaos, criticism of the children's homework, and arguments about money and drinking.

As we progressed to the eighth grade, Sister Laurentia decided it was time to teach us civics, and we would hold class elections after lunch. It didn't take the boys long to realize that with 15 boys and 25 girls in our class that a girl would be president. The boys could not tolerate such a disaster, so a plan was formulated. I would run for president, and Albert was assigned as my campaign manager.

When we returned to afternoon classes, Sister Laurentia opened the floor for nominations. Albert raised his hand and nominated me. After recording this on the blackboard, she asked for additional nominations. Albert raised his hand again and nominated Geraldine Sawyer. Sister looked a little quizzical but confirmed that in a democratic society, you can nominate more than one candidate. So, she recorded Geraldine's name and asked if there were any more nominees. Albert was not finished. By the end of the nominations, there were six girl candidates. The vote was taken, and the boy's candidate won in a landslide. Wearing my orange Captain Marvel sweatshirt, I assumed the responsibility of this important office.

Since it was close to Christmas, the first order of business for this administration was to plan the decorations for our classroom. To soothe the feathers of the opposing political factions, the president volunteered that Albert and I would provide a Christmas tree for the classroom. Sister Laurentia thought that it was a lovely gesture in the true spirit of the season. After we left school that day, Albert asked me how we were going to accomplish this since we had no money. The president had a plan, though.

Sears & Roebuck had an outdoor garden shop where they sold Christmas trees during the holidays. It was bordered by an eight-foot chain link fence. I explained to Albert that, if a tree accidentally fell over the fence, someone could pick it up and cross the street and enter a park. On the other side of the park was Lockhart Street and in a matter of a few minutes, the tree could be at St. Mary's. From the moral perspective, since the tree was going to a Catholic school, this would certainly not be a sin.

Albert was the inside man, and I was the outside man. Sister Laurentia was ecstatic with the beautiful tree and when Sister Otillia was notified, she seemed very pleased because they both knew that my older brother had entered the seminary. Perhaps this was a turning point in my life and my redemption had arrived. Here I was, eight years into this, and the sisters still didn't understand me.

Graduation was in June and shortly after, the Tempert family moved from the Northside, and I did not see Albert again for fifty years.

As mentioned earlier, if you wanted some spending money growing up on the Northside of Pittsburgh, you had to figure out a way to earn it. One of the easiest ways was to go from door to door and offer to return soda or milk bottles to the local grocery store. The return rate was two cents for a soda or milk bottle and five cents for a quart soda bottle.

During World War II, all activities on the home front were dedicated to supporting the war effort. Scrap drives were begun. Since Joe Panyi and I had wagons, we would search the neighborhood for scrap metal and take it to the salvage yard. We were paid by the pound for what we collected.

A third source of income was excess cooking grease. This item was a component of some explosives, and when delivered to Al Gumm's Butcher Shop, this would result in additional cash.

3
NEW
HORIZONS

BREAKOUT FROM THE NORTHSIDE

The 1940's were fading into the rearview mirror, and the 1950's were coming on with major technological advances. Television brought the Lone Ranger and Tonto into our living rooms. The auto industry offered air conditioning in luxury cars like the Packard and the Cadillac. Arnold Palmer changed golf so that it became a game for the common man and not just the wealthy. Our county became engaged in another war in an obscure part of the world called Korea.

The summer between finishing grade school and starting high school provided ample time to play baseball. All the neighborhood boys would pack a lunch and head to Fineview field. The field had been a storage lot for a now defunct brick foundry. The infield had fragments of bricks sticking up at various places. This made every ground ball an adventure. The outfield walls were cliffs that were approximately fifty feet high.

We always played a doubleheader. The routine was to play a morning game and then have lunch. For several consecutive days when lunchtime came, my lunch had disappeared. To solve this problem, one morning I prepared a sandwich with Dash dogfood and mayonnaise. Leaving it on a bench, it disappeared as planned. When the second game was about the start, an announcement was made from home plate as to the contents of said sandwich. Eddie Werner, the neighborhood blimp, was already in the field at first base. He promptly ran behind the stands to hurl his meal into a trash can. After that, my sandwiches remained secure.

Another sports highlight came one day when I was catching (yes, you can put on a catcher's mask while wearing glasses). Jeff Higgins was pitching. The batter up was Lefty Klenk, a few years older than most of the players. Lefty had already established himself as a three-sport athlete in high school. To calm my pitcher down, I went to the mound and assured him that Lefty could not catch up to his fastball.

Returning to the catcher's position, the signal was given for the fastball and it came right down the middle. What a sensational result! I had never seen a baseball hit that far in all my life. Three hundred feet down the right field line, fifty feet above the cliff, across the street, and as it was still rising, it hit the second story of a house. If it had been any solace to the pitcher, Lefty went on to Purdue to play tight end on their football team.

"How cool can you be?"

Since my brother had been a four-year honor student at North Catholic High School and had just finished his novitiate year in the Marianist Order, the Brothers of Mary greeted me warmly. My homeroom teacher was Brother

Robert Backherms. On the first day of class, I had the strange feeling that I had seen him somewhere before. That evening, a review of the novitiate class picture showed him standing next to my brother. This was his first assignment! Triumphantly, I showed the picture to my mother and she agreed. She also added that if I gave that information to any of my classmates, it would be big trouble for me.

Brother Backherms was short, enthusiastic, and a strict taskmaster. He was a superb teacher and gave me an excellent basic approach to learning that served me well in my lifetime. He also taught Latin both to the first- and second-year students.

Since our freshman class had 250 students, there was no place on the football team for a scrawny kid with thick glasses. This was just as well because with studies and work, I had little time for any practices. My first job after-school hours was as a soda jerk at Holt's Dairy Store on East Ohio Street. The pay was forty cents an hour. Shortly after starting, a twenty-five per cent raise took it to fifty cents an hour. During the summer, I cut grass at St. Mary's Cemetery on Mount Troy Road. Almost all the headstones had German names, some dating back to the early 1800's.

The next year, C.J. told me of an opening as a bowling pinsetter at St. Mary's Lyceum, the men's club in our parish. The pay was ten cents a line, but if you worked fast, you could do five lines at a time and get in five games an hour. This was a step up the economic ladder. However, the big advantage was that after the bowling was finished, it was possible to go into the card room and pool hall. My pin-setting partner was John Piorkowski. We would take our evening earnings and enter the poker game and/or the pool competition. Since the bowlers had been consuming beer all evening, it was not too difficult to add to our nightly earnings. We continued this for several months until reports of the members losing ten to twenty dollars filtered back to the president of the club, my grandfather. An edict was then issued that underage non-members were not permitted to gamble on the premises.

Since football and basketball were beyond my capabilities, I jumped at the opportunity to compete in a boxing tournament. Representing 11-A in the intramurals, I was matched in the 118-122-pound division. I thought this was going to be easy, since my opponent had to be a featherweight. When the bell rang for the first round, my opponent came charging across the ring like a madman. To defend myself, I ducked my head and put my left arm straight out. He ran right into it and to both of our surprise, he ended up sitting on the canvas! The fight was stopped, and my athletic career was launched with a first-round TKO.

So now, onto the championship bout for the featherweight division. Bobby Baker was the opponent. He had the reputation for being one mean little son of a gun. All of my classmates turned out for the bout. During the introductions, I properly acknowledged my fans. The bell rang and after sparring around for a minute, he sent a left jab to the midsection. Instinctively, I blocked the punch. The next thing I saw was a right cross heading for my nose. Flashing lights immediately followed. My boxing skills told me to grab him and go into a clinch for a few seconds to clear my head. This I did until the referee broke the clinch. Dancing back with my guard up, I saw blood on his cheek and shoulder. I smelled blood! I was ready for the kill!

There was only one problem. I had not laid a glove on him. That had to be my blood. The referee stepped in to stop the fight. Since all my classmates were there, I began to protest the decision, being careful not to protest too much so the referee would reverse his decision. This ended my high school athletic career with two spectacular first-round knockouts.

Tommy T. became my after-school companion during this time and we wandered the city streets together. He taught me how to drive at age 14 and also the benefits of capitalism.

He had the habit of borrowing various cars when he knew that the owners would not be using them. One lesson he taught me was that Packards were more durable than taxicabs. One evening after his uncle had retired for the night, he borrowed his uncle's beautiful black 1949 Packard sedan. We went for a ride out Perrysville Avenue. Since it had the newest option, automatic transmission, he wanted to demonstrate how easily it handled.

As we were returning back to the Northside, it was necessary to turn left onto Perrysville Avenue. Apparently, Tommy's driving skills had not progressed to the use of turn signals, and he turned directly into the path of an oncoming yellow cab. The Packard performed beautifully, hitting the cab head on and pushing it directly back from whence it came. At this point, Tommy continued to further demonstrate his driving skills by flooring the Packard as we left the cab in a cloud of steam from its ruptured radiator. Later that week, Tommy informed me that his uncle could not figure out how a yellow cab could have backed up that hard into his parked car to do so much damage!

In addition to his driving skills, Tommy had a natural ability as a mechanic. So, we went into the auto repair business. My sister Jeanie's boyfriend, Dick Gaffney, needed the windshield replaced on his car, and I assured him we could handle this. This successful project led us to our next customer. Regis Strahler, a friend of my Uncle Bob's, had a 1940 Pontiac that hadn't run for several months. Well, Tommy was able to get it started, but unfortunately it sounded like eight woodpeckers on steroids!

The obvious diagnosis was that it had sticky valves. So, H & T Auto Repair came to the rescue. I read the directions to Tommy and he did the work. Mr. Strahler was ecstatic. Three weeks later, the Pontiac was towed to his house, and we never did see it running again.

The entrepreneurship lesson was more complicated but no less exciting. It was illegal to sell fireworks in the State of Pennsylvania. One day, Tommy informed me that it was possible to obtain fireworks by mail order from West Virginia. So, we placed an order and were shortly in business. The students at North Catholic High School were eager customers for this product. As the size of the orders grew, bonus fireworks were given to the middlemen by the manufacturer. Soon, our gym bags were laden with cherry bombs and firecrackers as we walked to school. The bonus gifts included more sophisticated items including aerial rockets.

Being ethical businessmen, we could not sell a product without first testing it. Therefore, one clear November night, we climbed up onto a railroad trestle where we could conduct a proper evaluation. Approximately 15-20 rockets were set securely to the roof of an empty boxcar. We wired them for successive ignition, lit the fuse, and hurried back down the trestle to watch the experience. The first rocket went off and soared high into the sky and bright red starbursts appeared, followed by an appropriate loud bang. We were ecstatic at our own success! There can, however, be too much of a good thing. Thirty seconds later, a second rocket went high into the sky, resulting in scintillating green flares and a similar loud blast. At this point, we realized that we had programmed another ten minutes of an aerial display for the Northside on a clear winter's evening.

It seemed prudent to distance ourselves from the scene. As we hurried up Cedar Avenue, we correctly predicted that the police cruisers speeding towards the railroad trestle would assume that two boys walking home with their gym bags from some athletic event would have no connection to the spectacular event.

Tommy dropped out of high school his second year. He was placed in a special school for boys who kept borrowing other people's cars without permission. Later on, he moved to Foley, Alabama, since there were other agencies in Pittsburgh who wanted to question him about these practices.

New friends and new vistas presented themselves as high school progressed. What led to my ultimate breakout from the Northside mentality was a summer job after my junior year at Liberty Motors. This was a Studebaker dealership at Liberty Avenue and the 31st Street Bridge. I was hired to wash and recondition used cars. My father was a salesman there and convinced Sam Liberto, the owner, to employ me for the summer. This was a fun job working with different cars every day. In the evenings, my father would drive home a "trade-in," and give me the keys to take it for a test drive. I was to evaluate the car and advise him what it needed to be ready for sale.

When the summer was over, I had saved enough money to buy my first car. It was a 1941 Chevy business coupe. The car was forest green with many rust spots. My after-school time was spent doing body work and filling in the rusted-out holes with Bondo. The next project was applying a light green paint to the roof in the latest style of the new 1952 Chevy Bel Air model. One complication was that the paint I used was leftover indoor paint, so that with the first rainfall, the car was a forest green below with light green stripes running down from the roof. It was a most unique appearance.

Now I could escape the Northside and expand my vistas. My new friends in high school became important to my mindset. Having fun and progressing towards a productive lifestyle were not incompatible. Plans for college and careers were topics of discussion during and after school, rather than how to avoid the police in our endeavors.

One area I could establish identity and self-esteem was in the academic arena. Without too much effort, I was able to make the honor roll each semester for all four years. At graduation, my ranking was second in a class of 225.

At this time in my life, my thinking turned toward what the future would bring. My skillset did not promise an athletic career, and there was certainly not a call to the priesthood. Turning to the Scriptures, (Matthew 25:14-30 and Luke 19: 12-27) and the parable of the talents, it became obvious my strengths were in the academic arena. So, with the directive from St. Matthew and St. Luke, I set out to develop my talents to the best of my ability.

My two sisters had distinguished themselves so well academically, that they were both able to attend Duquesne University on full scholarships. As their lives unfolded, they would both go on to earn doctorates in their respective fields. My brother gained his doctorate in theology while in the Marianist Order. For me to go to college would certainly require significant financial help.

My sisters always wanted to improve their little brother intellectually. They had pretty much thrown in the towel on improving my artistic sensibilities but still held out some hope for an academic scholarship. The testing at that time relied heavily on math and vocabulary. Basic math was a piece of cake for me. So, we concentrated on improving vocabulary. The test prep handout for vocabulary became my constant companion. We aimed for ten new words a day to be conquered at the dinner table.

Since Pittsburgh was a heavily industrialized city, it

was pretty much assumed by the high school counselors that if you were college-bound, it meant an engineering future. The top schools in the area were Carnegie Tech (now Carnegie Mellon) and the University of Pittsburgh. So, when the test for a scholarship at Carnegie Tech was offered, I applied to take it. When the results of the test were announced, I received a letter from the scholarship committee that I did not qualify for this award.

However, the test results were also used by the Gulentz scholarship committee to award scholarships to George-town University for students in Catholic high schools in the Pittsburgh Archdiocese. Indeed, I was awarded a full four-year room, board, and tuition scholarship. It was noted that usually only one scholarship was awarded each year, but there had been a tie on the test by two students. The committee had met, and since there were adequate funds, two boys were awarded scholarships for this year only. Michael Nee from Central Catholic High School was the other recipient.

Upon arriving at school that Monday morning, there was excitement at the bulletin board as the results were posted. My homeroom teacher, Fr. Horst, congratulated me, and then the vice principal, Brother Schick, stopped me in the hall to congratulate me. It was the first time that it was not for disciplinary reasons.

I was too embarrassed to tell anyone that I did not know

where Georgetown University was located or what type of curriculum they offered. After visiting the library, I learned that it was located in Washington, D.C. and the school did not offer an engineering degree. The scholarship was established by Charles Gulentz, a steel magnate. He had passed away, but his widow still lived in Pittsburgh.

Mrs. Gulentz hosted a luncheon each spring to meet the new scholars and to introduce them to prior scholarship recipients. This was held at the posh Schenely Hotel during the Easter break. It was the first time I had ever attended such an elegant affair, dressed in my only suit. I met a charming and slightly built gray-haired lady who was quite interested in her scholars. As I was leaving the hotel, I noticed her standing in the lobby. Since it was drizzling outside, I inquired if she had a ride home. She said she had called for her car and driver, but the switchboard at her apartment building was busy. So, I offered to drive her home.

So now, we have the scrawny little kid with thick glasses driving the industrial magnate's widow up Fifth Avenue in his $35 1939 Buick coupe that had a hole in the muffler. Mrs. Gulentz pleasantly commented that she had never ridden in a hot rod before. As we approached the Clarion Arms Apartments, she directed me to pull up to the front entrance. As I stopped, a very officious man dressed in a uniform was peering out the door at the car. He obviously heard us coming. After a brief moment, he looked in the window and recognized my multi-millionaire passenger. He produced an umbrella from under his arm, opened the door with a "Good afternoon, Mrs. Gulentz. Be careful not to slip on the pavement." Thanking me for my kindness, she disappeared into the lobby as the doorman cast one more suspicious glance, probably to be certain that I vacated the premises promptly.

Obviously, the scholarship offers buoyed my self-esteem. I had learned that I could compete favorably at this level of competition. Additional scholarship offers came in from St. Vincent College in Latrobe, Pennsylvania as well as a partial and merit scholarship at the University of Pittsburgh.

As the school year progressed, my social life moved to Glenshaw, a quiet and affluent suburb. My new friends all grew up and went to grade school at St. Mary's, Pine Creek, which is a wonderful parish in which to raise a family. The friends I associated with in this area were all from very nurturing and substantial homes. Their fathers were lawyers, engineers, insurance executives, and a wonderful bread truck driver. The Lipkes, Bittners, Brogans, Glassos, Aquadros, and many others became part of my world. On the Northside of Pittsburgh, to be successful in life, all you had to do was to stay sober most of the time and stay out of jail.

Senior Prom with Marcia Killmeyer, 1953

Summer came and this year, I was employed at Wuslik Dodge where my father was now working. I was hired to be the porter, mopping and waxing the showroom floors and assisting with the used cars. Still, it was fun because I got to drive many different cars. Then one day about noon, my father asked me to drive him home. This was unusual because he always had a demonstrator to drive. I was told to be quiet and just get him out of there. Drinking had just claimed another job from him. To my surprise, I was able to continue working there for the rest of the summer.

Graduation North Catholic Class of 1953

Excitement was in the air as we neared the end of summer. Everyone was preparing for college except for one of my closest friends, Chuck Lipke. His father drove a truck for Town Talk bread. Chuck was the oldest of six children and there was just not enough money for college. Chuck had taken a full-time job and was able to pursue his education attending night school, working toward his degree. He was a bright young man and impressed everyone with how hard he worked.

Ed Bittner and Kerry Aquadro were headed to Pittsburgh for engineering. Vince Brogan went to St. Vincent College on a football scholarship. The more affluent Scholl twins, Nancy and Suzanne, were off to St. Mary's in South Bend, Indiana. The other girls in our group were still in high school.

This brings me to Chi-Chi. Her father was a prominent attorney in Pittsburgh who was running for district attorney. Her mother was a charming lady with a winning smile. As for Chi-Chi, an Italian beauty, she was extremely popular with the boys. Her aspiration was to become a great actress. When I first became associated with this circle of friends, she was Chuck's girlfriend. She and I hit it off as "just friends." Her mother may have encouraged this relationship with a young man who "just won a scholarship to Georgetown," as she would introduce me to members of their family. As the summer wore on, Chi-Chi's and Chuck's romance hit upon hard times, and I began to spend more time around her home.

One evening as we chatted in the front seat of my car, I told her that she reminded me of Gina Lollobrigida and that would certainly help in her theatrical future. She then asked if I usually took my glasses off when kissing a girl. Being the cosmopolitan type, my reply was, "Only if they are hot enough to steam up my glasses." Immediately, I realized this was a mistake! Girls mature more rapidly than boys. Italians have a reputation for being hot-blooded and the women are renowned for certain physical attributes. The glasses came off and there was no question in my mind that this was a major glandular mismatch. Fortunately, headlights turned into the long and winding driveway, and I was able to resume breathing. The summer winds of romance ended too soon, and then it was off to Georgetown and Washington, DC.

4

FASTER
COMPANY

The day after Labor Day in 1953, with a brand-new suitcase given to me by my sisters as a going away gift, I boarded a Greyhound bus heading for Washington, D.C. Sporting a crew cut and wearing a navy-blue suit, I felt very grown up. The trip was uneventful. Upon arriving in the D.C. bus station, I hailed a cab and asked to go to Georgetown University, also requesting that we drive past the White House on the way. That was an exciting way to begin a new adventure.

Upon entering the gates of Georgetown, we passed the statue of John Carroll, its founder, and arrived at the reception area for freshman students. Exiting the cab, I was greeted by an officious looking sophomore who escorted me to the registrar. After filling out the proper forms, I was asked if I would pay for the entire year's room, board, and tuition with one check. The total would be $1,600, a huge sum in those days. Since I had $80 (my total fortune) in my pocket and no checking account, I inquired as to where to go to pick up scholarship aid.

The name Gulentz produced a favorable response, and I was escorted to my new quarters by two other sophomores. My room was in Old Healy Hall, an ancient building named after a more ancient Jesuit. It was a single room on the fourth floor directly under the clock tower. It became immediately apparent that I would not need a watch since Old Healy gonged every 15 minutes 24 hours a day.

The room itself was six by fifteen with a bed, desk, and a chair. There was also a small closet. There was one window facing east, and when I looked out that first evening, I was able to see the brilliantly illuminated capitol building sitting on top of Capitol Hill. Pretty heady stuff for the scrawny little kid from the Northside of Pittsburgh.

It did not take long to unpack the one suitcase and since it was approaching dinnertime, I ventured out into the hallway to meet some of my new classmates. The freshman class came from all over the USA and had several foreign students. There was a hubbub of activity. Trunks were being carried into the dorm. Mothers were talking about putting up curtains and asking where a payphone was to make dinner reservations. When Old Healy gonged 6:00 pm, those of us who were not going to the Shoreham Hotel for dinner found the dining hall. This group included Ed Apen from Niagara Falls and Oscar Salvatierra from Tucson, Arizona. Later that evening and over the next few days, I met the rest of our dormmates. It was interesting how water seeks its own level and so do social and economic realities. Early bull sessions raged from getting one's Mercedes gull-wing roadster from Birmingham, Alabama to Washington, D.C. or taking over the family business in New York City. Another hot topic was, when was the first tea dance at Georgetown visitation?

The first Friday after the start of school brought an exodus from campus as several of my new classmates had to travel to Boston, New York, or other Eastern cities to play golf at their fathers' country clubs. That Monday morning, several new cars, including the Mercedes, appeared in the parking lot behind Old Healy.

Since there was no engineering degree offered at Georgetown, the plan was to get a B.S. (Bachelor of Science) in Chemistry. For this reason, many of my classes were with the pre-Med students. The conversations with these students were primarily about how to maintain a 2.5 GPA (grade point average, based on a 3.0 system) since this was the minimum to obtain admission to Georgetown's Medical School.

General chemistry presented no problem for me because the courses at North Catholic were geared to people going into chemical engineering. Other required courses such as German, Cosmology, and Philosophy did not invoke any interest. If you were classified 1-A for the draft, it was necessary to get into R.O.T.C. (Reserve Officers' Training Corps) to defer the call to active duty.

World War II necessitated a military draft for all able-bodied males between the ages of 18 and 38. Mandatory military service continued until 1973. So, if an eligible male wanted to continue his education, he had to request a deferment every step along the way. Since I was classified 1-A in high school, that meant several different programs were necessary for my participation from that day I graduated from high school through the completion of my residency in ophthalmology.

The Air Force R.O.T.C. program seemed the most attractive, and I applied and was issued an ill-fitting uniform. In addition, the cadets were given an overcoat that must've been a leftover from a Siberian campaign. We were then sent to the drill field to learn close-order drill. Marching was not high on the list of important things for pre-med and Chemistry majors. However, there was never a shortage of Air Force brass in the D.C. area who wanted to come and inspect troops.

This does not sound like much unless you are the shortest cadet in the formation and, therefore, the logical one for the general to personally inspect. This also does not sound too difficult, unless you are wearing a heavy woolen overcoat and knit gloves. The concept was to release the bolt of the rifle with your left thumb and hand the weapon to the general. Our unit commander did not find it humorous to hand my rifle to the general with a knit glove caught in the bolt mechanism.

When the first six weeks' grade period arrived, notice was given to me that a B average was necessary for maintaining a scholarship. Thank the heavens for an A in Chemistry. This did serve notice that the other courses needed to be taken seriously. Since the Mercedes and the other new cars were busy driving young ladies about town, that left only pre-meds studying in the dorms. These guys had their act together and were serious students. As the school year progressed, it became evident that I could compete at this level.

Being warned about the academic requirements to maintain a scholarship, all class grades became important to me. This would include R.O.T.C. As an incentive to encourage careers in the Air Force, our instructor, Colonel Ansel Wheeler, told the class that the top three scorers on the final exam would be taken to Andrews Air Force Base and would take control of an actual plane in flight.

Vince Caruso, who became a fighter pilot, Johnny Bright, who became a military cargo pilot, and Harry Brady, who got air sick, were the lucky winners. One sunny day, we were taken to the air base and into the pilots' ready room. Of course, we were in uniform and needed to change into flight jackets.

My uniform was ill-fitting, and the pants were several inches too long. To solve that problem, I used bright yellow suspenders to hold the pants almost up to my armpits. When the colonel saw this, he asked me who I thought I was. My reply was, "Steve Canyon." Steve Canyon was a comic strip, swashbuckling Air Force major who did all sorts of heroic things. My classmates thought that was a brilliant response. But the colonel was not as thrilled. The day was somewhat of a success, however, since I did not vomit on the controls during the five minutes in the cockpit.

Bill Slagel, a high school friend, joined the Marines rather than going to college. He had the chiseled face and build of the movie star Gregory Peck. Not surprisingly, the Marines assigned him to the Honor Guard at Arlington National Cemetery. Bill called me one day and asked if I wanted to play golf. Neither of us had any golf equipment, but he said that he would take care of things.

We drove up to the gate of this gorgeous country club where a Military Police Officer came out of the guard house. Bill showed him his ID and we were waved on to the pro shop. The sign above the door read, "Welcome to the Congressional Country Club." So now the scrawny kid from the Northside of Pittsburgh is going to play golf at the private club where the presidents of the United States and congressmen are members.

We entered the pro shop and were assigned a cart and given golf clubs and a generous supply of balls. The pro pointed us to the locker room where he said we could change our shoes. Well, neither of us had golf shoes, but we entered the locker room anyway. Once again, I was overwhelmed by its opulence.

We proceeded to play 18 holes, and with some judicious cheating, we both broke 140.

On the home front, things were not going well. One evening, my mother called to tell me that my grandmother, Rosie, had suffered a stroke that morning and had passed away. There was no money to fly me home for the funeral and I was down to my last five dollars. I did not get back to Pittsburgh.

My father was still drifting from job to job and obviously alcohol played a prominent part in this. My sisters were planning a double wedding in the spring, and there would be no alcohol permitted in the house during this event. The school year progressed and to pick up some extra cash, each week night, I started a catering service to the local deli, to bring back late-night nourishment for late-night studying.

For my sisters' wedding, I was sent a ticket to fly back

home, my first time ever, on a commercial airplane. The weddings went off as planned with two beautiful brides and two handsome grooms. I knew Bill Flaherty and Dick Gaffney well and was very pleased that my sisters had married such good men. The 'no alcohol' ban worked for most of the day, but shortly after the reception, at our house, my father slipped off for a few quick belts.

When it came time to drive some of the guests home, it was suggested that I do this. My father was back working at Wuslik Motors, so I had a new Dodge to drive. On the way home, I stopped at a light on East Ohio Street, right in front of Wuslik Motors. The owner, Nick Wuslik, stepped out in front of the car and demanded that I pull immediately into their driveway. I did and explained that I was driving a guest home from the reception. He demanded the keys, and my father lost another job due to alcohol.

After the school year, I returned home. Since I had now decided to switch to pre-med, it was necessary to take organic chemistry at Pitt that summer so that I could take a required Biology course that fall back at Georgetown. Fortunately, I was able to get part-time work as a census taker for the city directory.

Working for the Reuben H. Donnelly Company as a census taker was not the most cerebral activity. Each morning, when reporting for work, the census takers were issued street names and addresses and totally blank information cards and sent out to ring doorbells. When the names of each individual residing at that address were recorded manually on the blank card, it was required to record everyone's occupation and other salient information. When the cards were returned to the supervisor that afternoon, the information would be checked against the last year's directory and the appropriate changes would be made.

After a few days on the job, it dawned on me that 99% of the people who lived in Pittsburgh did not move every year. The old directory was 99% accurate. Therefore, if the census taker went to the library first and used last year's directory, it was possible to fill out the forms much more efficiently than ringing every doorbell.

The way to pick up changes was to go to the corner bar or grocery store. Most bartenders were more than happy to review the year's prior changes with me. If there was no place of business on the corner, it was easy enough to walk through the neighborhood until one of the residents would be outside their home and announce that the census taker was there. Once they confirmed their data, it seemed logical to ask if Paul and Sophie and their three children still lived next door. In the stable, blue-collar neighborhoods of Pittsburgh, it was possible to do an entire block in ten minutes.

Since my father's reputation had gotten around all the auto dealerships in town, he had difficulty getting employment as an auto salesman. He did gain employment, however, as a census taker. His production was much slower than mine due to my stop at the library and his stops at each bar.

One of my interesting stops was on the lower Northside. Upon ringing the bell, the door was opened by a woman with fiery red hair and dressed in a royal blue flowing silk robe. As instructed, I announced that the census taker was here and presented my credentials. It was a bit of a surprise that there were five or six young women there. They all had cutesy first names like Bambi and Cookie. However, none of them offered a surname. When we got to the question of occupation, there was some deep thought and finally I was informed they were all entertainers. So now we have the scrawny little kid who used to observe life from his front steps taking the census at the local whorehouse!

The summer ended uneventfully and it was back to school. Mike Nee, the other Gulentz scholar, and I had become such good friends our freshman year that we decided to room together for this year. The choosing of dorm rooms in the sophomore year was allotted by the combined class rank of the combined two roommates. Mike and I received the second pick. Future Supreme Court

Justice Antonin Scalia and his roommate had first choice. The sophomore dorm was the renovated old Georgetown Hospital and the two largest rooms were the two former operating rooms. We chose one with our own sinks and hot and cold running water. Sam Moran and Bud Bardana chose the other.

Shortly after the sophomore year began, news came that my father had disappeared again. No one seemed to know where he was. One afternoon several weeks later, I received a postcard from my father that he was in a hospital in Wheeling, West Virginia, undergoing treatment for alcoholism.

In those days, many people did not consider alcoholism a disease, but rather a sign of moral turpitude. In any event, I conveyed his whereabouts to my mother and added that he would be returning to Pittsburgh in a few weeks. For reasons that I do not understand and neither of my parents ever discussed, he never had another drink in his life.

This event led me to consider my relationship to alcohol. My first encounter was on New Year's Eve as a freshman in high school. Tommy T's mother was going out to a friend's house and would be staying the night. Tommy and I were going to stay in their apartment and watch Guy Lombardo at midnight play "Enjoy Yourself, It's Later Than You Think."

We found a bottle of red wine in the kitchen and decided to sample it. We drank the whole bottle within about fifteen minutes and decided to visit some young ladies who were having a party. We were such big shots! This went well until we began to throw up what appeared to be dark red blood. We were promptly invited to leave and return to Tommy's to suffer together. This cooled my interest in alcohol until late high school when all my contemporaries began to drink beer. This seemed an innocuous activity and did not lead to any problems.

At Georgetown, the sophisticates drank the hard stuff and martinis were the rage. It did not take me long to learn that at 120 pounds, my capacity was not that of a 240-pound linebacker. With the family history and these facts, it behooved me to be ever-vigilant in regard to this disease.

The remainder of the sophomore year was uneventful, and I returned to Pittsburgh for the summer. The census job was available, and they were happy to have me back since I was much more productive than any of the other census takers.

The next school year flew past and the only thing of note was that I had my own radio show at WGTN at 6:30 pm. Basically, it was just a disc jockey show, but it was a lot of fun. The summer following the junior year, Frank Garrison, the best man at Jeanie and Dick's wedding, got me a job at Stouffer's Restaurant. This was a most interesting job since it required my working each full-time employees' vacation days. This, in essence, allowed me to learn all the jobs in a restaurant from working on the loading dock, the steam table, dishwashing and opening up the breakfast bar at 6:30 am If the coffee was not hot and ready by that time, there would be some very unhappy customers.

That summer I taught Mike how to drive, and he bought a 1950 Pontiac and drove it back to school. When Thanksgiving break came, the plan was to drive back to Pittsburgh. Sam Moran and Dave Morton were going to ride with us. Sam was a pre-med from Oil City, Pennsylvania and Dave, a pre-law student from Philadelphia. They both were meeting their parents in Pittsburgh. We headed northwest out of D.C. toward the Pennsylvania Turnpike. We stopped at a roadside diner for chili and coffee. As we left the diner, it started to sleet. I offered to drive, but Mike said he felt good after the break. After about 45 minutes, as we were going to a higher elevation near the turnpike, conditions began to deteriorate. The road was two-lane blacktop – which turned out to be black ice – and the car went into a skid as we encountered a dip in the road. Sam yelled, "Look out!"

We skidded across directly into the path of a tractor trailer coming down the hill. I was napping in the right front seat and awakened to see the front wheel of the truck smashing into the front driver's side of the car. The impact spun the car around, and I was thrown out the right front door. Seatbelts had not yet been introduced as a safety feature. The car began rolling down the hill and my left front leg was caught between the floor and the door post.

Now, I was face down being dragged along the highway. I could not move my leg, so grasping it with both hands, I was able to pull it free from the still moving car. As I laid on the highway unable to move because of the pain in my leg, suddenly, it was eerily quiet and totally black. The snowflakes were falling on my face.

After a little while, I heard some voices and I called out for help. Someone came by and put a tarpaulin over me. My glasses had come off during the collision, and I asked the man with the tarp if he would look for them. Within a minute or two, he returned with the undamaged glasses. I'm not sure how long I laid on the roadway until the sirens announced the arrival of the ambulances. I was placed on a stretcher on my side in the ambulance facing away from another stretcher that was already there. I could not roll over because of the pain, but I could hear some very labored breathing.

I asked one of the attendants how the other people were. He said two of the occupants were killed instantly and the third one was in the ambulance with us and was in bad shape. I asked him to describe the other person in the ambulance with me. The only description he gave was that he had red hair. I knew immediately it was Mike.

After about 25 minutes, we arrived at Bedford Hospital, a rural hospital near the turnpike. They removed Mike from the ambulance, and I knew things were not good as his breathing had become more labored with gurgling sounds. Then I was taken to another room where it was determined that my injuries were not life-threatening.

The police, and then a Catholic priest, came in. The police wanted the names and information of the other three people in the car. The chaplain informed me that Mike had died shortly after arriving in the ER. A nurse came in and said she would give me a shot for the pain. I asked if they would call my family on the telephone and let me speak to them first. When my mother got on the phone, I told her the sad story and emphasized that even though I was banged up, there was no head injury, and I had been conscious the entire time.

After the call was over, the nurse gave me a shot of morphine and the doctor began to sew up my lacerations. Next stop was radiology. Then everything faded into a blur as the narcotic did its work. The next morning, it was confirmed that my left femur was in three pieces and would require prompt surgery, but none of the doctors at Bedford Hospital were qualified to do this. They also said my left knee had been severely injured and would require surgery at a later date.

Another shot of morphine and then it was off to the Allegheny Hospital in Pittsburgh. Shortly after arrival, I was seen by Dr. Robert Botkin, an orthopedic surgeon, and was scheduled for surgery the next morning. The femur was repaired with an 18-inch intramedullary pin and several screws to connect all three pieces together.

The most difficult part of the ordeal was meeting the parents of my three friends and relating the story to them.

I was hospitalized for two weeks and then it was home until after the Christmas holidays. My high school friends were great about visiting me at the hospital and at home. My former boss at Stouffer's Restaurant sent me a catered New York strip steak while I was still in the hospital.

By mid-January, I was able to return to school and take the exams and scored a cumulative B plus for the semester. Sam's roommate, Bud Bardana, and I roomed together for the remainder of the year. With Bud and Don Dowler supplying the muscle, I was pushed to classes in a wheelchair.

Graduation was in early June and I was able to walk across the stage on crutches to receive the diploma. As a side note, I was seated next to Antonin Scalia, having no idea where he was headed. We were both in the front row with all the dignitaries, he because he was the valedictorian, and me because I could not bend my broken leg.

Georgetown Graduation, 1957 – with my parents

The parents of my deceased friends elected to sue the trucking company since there was no evidence of any skid marks on the roadway. Our family did not participate in the lawsuit since my feeling was that the truckdriver had no chance at all to respond to our crossing into his lane. What this all meant was I had to return to the scene of the accident and reconstruct it for the plaintiffs' attorney.

Viewing the mangled Pontiac at the service station lot within a mile of the accident was exceedingly difficult. The steel dashboard where my leg had impacted was dented at least six inches. It made me realize that I was fortunate to still have a left leg. Testifying in court also kept the event fresh in my mind. For several years, I would awake during the night to see the front wheel of the tractor-trailer entering the driver's compartment of the Pontiac. The first trial ended in a mistrial decision by the judge. A second trial ended with a decision for the defense.

It was this time in my life that questions about my religion began. People would tell me that, "God has saved you for some greater good." How could a loving God allow three young men to die and let me live? I could not ascribe any religious significance to my survival. My best rationalization was the secular answer that, "God had nothing to do with it. It just happened that way."

Prior to the accident, I had been hired by a catering company to be a waiter at Dwight D. Eisenhower's Inaugural Ball. Needless to say, I was unable to keep this commitment.

While still at home after Christmas, I called the dean's office at the University of Pittsburgh to find out if I was accepted to their medical school. Georgetown University Medical School had already offered me a spot for their upcoming year. However, they required a non-refundable deposit of $500 by the first of the year. $500 was major money for me, and I needed a response from Pitt. However, at the time, the dean had chicken pox! Explaining my dilemma to his secretary, she agreed to break with protocol and assured me of the acceptance. She said the dean would send out the official notice when he returned to work.

That summer was relatively uneventful. Due to the broken leg, I was unable to get a job. However, our parish church raffled off a new car every Labor Day. Selling chances in front of Sears provided some spending money. All Catholics know that chances are one dollar per chance and a book of six was five dollars. Therefore, for each six chances, the seller gets to keep one dollar.

That summer, I met an attractive young lady named Pidge (which certainly sounded better than Thelma). At a family picnic, she informed my mother how nice it would be to marry a doctor. Millie freaked out over this since we did not have a clue how medical school would be financed. After assuring my mother that it was Pidge's idea and not mine and that we had not even remotely discussed that prospect, Millie calmed down. Through some political channels, we were able to obtain a partial senatorial scholarship. That, with my working various part-time jobs during the school year, would suffice. As my mother said, no matter what the challenges, "we will manage" and we always did.

5
MEDICAL
SCHOOL

AND A VERY SOPHISTICATED YOUNG LADY

That September, my medical career began on a cane. The paranoia of medical students was legendary, and our class was no exception. The professors gave us the impression that students were academic fodder. On our first day, we were paired up in groups of four in the Gross Anatomy Lab. We named our cadaver 'Elmer' and he became part of our lives for the rest of the year. As the year progressed, Elmer became somewhat ripe, despite the formaldehyde. The four students assigned to Elmer were Fred Brown, a super WASP, (White Anglo-Saxon Protestant), Sid Lewis, a fallen-away Catholic, Bob Brougher, whose two older brothers and father were doctors, and me. Certainly, an unlikely group who became the best of friends working together to assure our academic survival.

Of the 101 entering freshman students, one quit school after the first Gross Anatomy Lab, and by the end of the year, we were down to 90 remaining students. It was a difficult year, but one that I could immerse myself in, this unbelievable, interesting academic pursuit. Gross Anatomy, Philosophy, Histology and Biochemistry required more study than any of my previous courses.

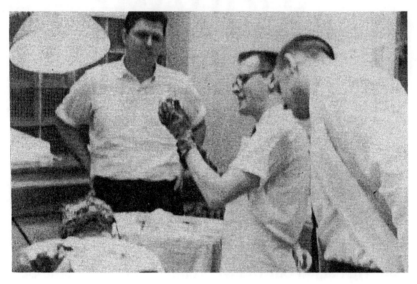

"Of course I know what I'm doing."

It was also a time when the most important event of my life took place. Fred Brown, Sid Lewis's wife, and Bob Brougher's wife, decided that I was not dating the right girls. Fred was dating Audrey Clark, whose roommate was Shirley Martin. Both Fred and Audrey were Protestants and neither of them knew many Catholics. So, Fred arranged a blind date for me. He felt that he was matching a couple who were made for each other. As young adults, we had discussed the upcoming election for almost a year ahead of the election because a Catholic (John F. Kennedy) could actually be president. When Fred and Audrey realized that Shirley and I were both planning on voting Republican, Fred set up our first date which started at Audrey and Shirley's apartment in fashionable Mount Lebanon.

After being introduced to the very sophisticated and attractive Miss Martin, we sat down to a repast of salad and spaghetti. I was immediately in awe of Miss Martin's charm and beauty and my only recollection of the meal was the massive mound of spaghetti that was served. It was piled so high that it was necessary to lean to the side of the table to see the person sitting across from me. When I asked if the Italian Olympic eating team was also coming to dinner, it didn't elicit the laughter that I had expected. Then it was off to see *To the Point,* a musical comedy about the founding and growth of Pittsburgh. The evening was quite successful and inexpensive since Fred had been given the tickets.

A week or so later, I called Miss Martin and set up a second date. This time, it was a semi-disaster. Driving my $25 1949 Hudson, we went to a par-3 golf course, and as we played, Miss Martin would puff on a cigarette and cough, hit the golf ball, puff on the cigarette and cough. This went on for 18 holes. She did not appear overly appreciative of my comments. "Did you ever think that if you didn't smoke so much that you would not cough so much?"

When she returned to their apartment that night, she informed her roommate that she would never go out with someone who had the gall to criticize her choices to smoke or not to smoke. Needless to say, this budding romance cooled off precipitously. A few months later, our fraternity planned a formal dance, and I called Miss Martin to invite her. The response was that she did not have a formal dress that she could fit into. I did not know if this was a put-off or that she had become chunky. In any event, I did not call her for several months, and she was not about to call me. When the school year ended, I called her and told her that I hoped that she would have a pleasant visit with her family in St. Louis.

The following evening, Fred Brown arrived at my doorstep in his aqua and white 1955 Chevrolet convertible and said he was driving to Atlantic City for the summer. I packed my suitcase, said goodbye to my mother and off we went on another adventure. We arrived on a Friday night and found a place to stay in a rooming house three blocks from the Boardwalk.

Saturday morning, we went to a pancake house where we knew several girls from Pittsburgh were working as waitresses. Since Fred had a check from his father for several hundred dollars and I had $15 in my wallet, it behooved me to find prompt employment. One of the waitresses, Winnie Brosious, mentioned that there was an opening for a busboy at Stouffer's Gaslight Club on the Boardwalk. After breakfast, I strolled down the Boardwalk and came to an upscale restaurant.

On entering, I was greeted by the hostess. I said I was there for the job. She seemed surprised that I was there for the waiter job because they had only fired him the night before. She advised me that I would need a white shirt, dark trousers, a cummerbund and a black bow tie. If I had them, I could start at four pm that afternoon. She gave me a menu that I could familiarize myself with and off I went to the nearest pawn shop to buy the required cummerbund and black bow tie. After the pawn shop, it was back to the pancake house to get a crash course from Winnie on how to wait on tables.

That evening, my first assignment was at table number one by the front door. My first customer was a man who ordered a Manhattan and a lobster dinner. After placing the order for a whole lobster, I walked back to the front of the restaurant where the customer waved me over to bring him another Manhattan. By the time his lobster arrived, he was well-oiled. As I sauntered back to where some of the waiters were standing, I thought that this job would be really easy. A few minutes later, one of the servers came back and asked, "Who has table number one? Your customer needs some help."

Being very conscientious, I hurried back to the table to see what was needed. The customer was sitting in place with the lobster in the middle of the table. A baked potato was on the floor along with several of the utensils and his napkin. The owner of the whole lobster was pounding with a spoon on the shell of one of the lobster's tails. I discreetly picked up the baked potato and demonstrated how to open the lobster shell with a nutcracker. He ordered another Manhattan, finished his dinner and left a five-dollar tip. This job proved ideal for a young person trying to recharge his batteries after a hard school year.

Working 4:00 pm to midnight allowed daily time on the beach, good money (several hundred dollars a week) and my only real sun tan. Fred got a job playing the piano at a cocktail lounge. Winnie's boyfriend, another classmate of ours, showed up and moved in with us for the rest of the summer.

School resumed after Labor Day and my interest in medicine grew daily. Soon we were taking histories and starting physical diagnostics. As soon as we began dealing directly with patients, medical school went from being an academic pressure cooker to a fun-filled learning experience. Since Bob Brougher's two brothers had gone through medical school at Pittsburgh, they knew which services were the best to apply for. Three specific instances are of note during the clinical years.

The first one involved Miss Martin, since she was being wined and dined by several of the eligible bachelors in the area. It became necessary to plan something to really impress her. The big day was a college football game, dinner, and a fraternity party that night. With eight dollars budgeted for this extravaganza, a student ID card was borrowed from a female classmate to get into the football stadium. This part of the plan worked beautifully as Pitt beat Notre Dame 13 to 7.

What to do next regarding dinner? An urgent call to my mother to bring a friend home for dinner proved to be another smashing success. When my mother met Miss Martin, she gave out a great sigh of relief, considering some of the young ladies that had preceded her. The eight dollars in my pocket was enough for the fraternity party at Frankie Gustine's Bar. Frankie was the second baseman for the Pirates. He also played for the Chicago Cubs later in his career. The spectacular end of this day was Miss Martin and Fred Brown doing the Charleston on the bar.

The second incident was the major disaster drill for the City of Pittsburgh. As part of the first aid class, we were assigned in groups of three to be the victims of this disaster. My group was to report to the triage nurse at the entrance to the football stadium. It was a cold, rainy morning and she told us our assignment was to go to the 50-yard line and lie down there and wait to be rescued. After about 15 minutes in the rain, the three of us concluded that we could be rescued just as easily at the Cozy Bar just down the street. The conclusion of this episode was that we were never rescued and received a D in first aid, my only D in medical school.

A third incident occurred during a Psychiatry lecture. Suddenly, I began having chest pains, difficulty breathing and a strange feeling in my trachea. When the lecture was over, I walked across the street to the emergency room of Presbyterian Hospital. There, the diagnosis of spontaneous pneumothorax (collapsed lung) was made, followed by an immediate admission.

Within an hour, a chest tube had been inserted (ouch!) and it was connected to an underwater seal. With each breath, a sharp stabbing pain indicated that the lung was re-expanding, forcing air bubbles into the water seal.

My first call was to my parents' house and my father answered the phone. After explaining the situation to him, I got down to the real business of my call. He needed to call Shirley Martin, Glenda Lackey, and Joan Smolko to let them know that I would be unable to keep my appointments with them later that week. The lung re-collapsed and, 48 hours later, a second chest tube was inserted and healing then progressed rapidly.

As every athlete knows, it is better to be lucky than good. This also applies to medical students. The following week, we started our surgical rotation. As part of the surgical training, each student is to sit in an amphitheater at a table with three surgeons who question him on various surgical problems. Seated around the amphitheater were my classmates observing the beleaguered student being peppered with questions by the inquisitors. As luck would have it, the case the surgeons presented to me was that of a young healthy male who developed sudden chest pain, shortness of breath and a shift of the trachea after no apparent physical activity. Yours truly received an A for a brilliant discussion of spontaneous pneumothorax.

Employment prospects improved in conjunction with my improving mobility. The summer between my second and third year was spent working for the school of public health on a research project about staph infections in the newborn nursery. Horace Gezon, M.D. was the project director and he was kind enough to let me be lead author in our publication in the Journal of Pediatrics.

The following summer was spent working for the Allegheny County Health Department skin testing in rural communities to determine the incidence of histo-plasmosis. These jobs were a step up the economic ladder and allowed me to buy a much more expensive car, a 1954 Plymouth for $125.

The Plymouth brings Miss Martin back into the narrative. The Lederle Drug Company invited our entire senior class to visit their facility in White Plains, New York, with a two-night stay in Manhattan. The wives and/or a guest were also invited to attend. Miss Martin, a trendsetter in fashion and sophistication, accepted my invitation. John Hodapp, another classmate, was also going so he and I roomed together as did Shirley and his guest.

The next item on the agenda was transportation and the Plymouth got the call. The car was mechanically sound but had a few issues. The cloth seats were torn and filthy. My mother had just replaced heavy maroon brocade drapes in our living room and these made for beautiful seat covers. Remember that "beauty is in the eye of the beholder."

Another issue was there was no trunk lock, and the trunk had to be secured by a rope that came through the trunk and was tied to an inside door handle. Upon arriving at the hotel in downtown Manhattan, the doorman came out to unload our luggage. Miss Martin dashed into the lobby because she was aware the difficulty the doorman would encounter. I graciously demonstrated the opening mechanism to him and joined Miss Martin at the registration desk. She should have realized then that if we married, our lives would be full of pleasant surprises such as this.

When Miss Martin told me that she definitely did not want my fraternity ring, I knew things were getting serious. We began to spend more and more time together. One evening while we were going out on a date, we had stopped by my parents' house so I could pick up a paycheck from one of my jobs. I took it to the neighborhood grocery store and cashed it.

Miss Martin politely asked if that was how I managed my finances. She expressed an opinion that she knew a better way to do this, and 56 years later, she still writes our checks and balances the checkbook.

As the school year progressed, the romance with Miss Martin blossomed, resulting in a proposal of marriage that fall. Miss Martin responded in typical manner, saying that she would take it under consideration and give me a response in due time.

Further inquiries on my part as to the status of the proposal revealed that she was making a chart listing the pros and cons in different columns while trying to reach a conclusion. It finally came down to an ultimatum on the suitor's part. Supposedly, the pros outweighed the cons. That evening at a party, we almost became unengaged as Miss Martin could not stop talking to the well-wishers until the middle of the night. I should've realized then that patience is a virtue in marriage.

Shirley's father was informed of the engagement and immediately scheduled a business trip to New York with a stopover in Pittsburgh. My meeting with Felix Martin was a very reassuring event to both of us and we got along very well from the start. The one exception was that I forgot where I had parked my car in a multi-level parking garage, but that was considered excusable since were both very nervous.

The wedding was set for June 24 in St. Louis. The last four months of school were a picnic since I had finished all the in-hospital rotations and therefore had only out-patient clinics, which required no night calls. My jobs during this time included doing pre-operative histories and physicals at St. Francis Hospital and also as night lab technician at West Penn Hospital. The latter job gave me room and meals at the hospital. I had money, a car, and a gorgeous fiancée, who now roomed with the president of the Models' Club of Pittsburgh. Suddenly, this increased my popularity with male classmates who frequently asked if I could get them a date. Life does not get any better than that!

It seemed as though the clinical years had flown by and graduation came June 17. Now it was off to St. Louis to begin our life together.

6
"SHIRLEY'S"
WEDDING

AND THE RAGIN' CAJUNS

Shirley left shortly after the graduation to return to her parents' home in St. Louis to finalize plans for the wedding. Since she had been living in Pittsburgh for several years, she did not want to have a large wedding and put that burden on her mother. The wedding which was always referred to as "Shirley's Wedding" was a small one with family and a few close friends.

My induction as an honorary Cajun began with Shirley's eleven-year-old sister, Mary Ann, bursting into the house screaming that there was a snake in the yard. After the commotion settled down, she proceeded to introduce me to her friend, Sally Frerking as, "This is the guy she is going to marry."

Shirley's parents were from Louisiana and were of

French descent. Felix's ancestors left France for a better life in Nova Scotia. As French Acadians, the families were banished from Nova Scotia because of their Catholic religion and were exiled to Louisiana. Felix Martin was a full-blooded Cajun (the word Acadian morphed into Cajun as the years went by.) Rena Fournet was not a Cajun and her family came from the Loire Valley in France. She was known as "Shine" because of her effervescent personality.

Felix was the son of a poor dirt farmer, and his mother died when he was less than two-years-old. After graduating from high school, using his basic intelligence and hard work, he became a self-made man. He attended college for a short time but did not graduate. However, by taking correspondence courses and by his reputation, he was rewarded with a degree in civil engineering. He rose to become the executive vice president of the Mississippi River Fuel Corporation.

Rena's father, a successful businessman in St. Martinsville, Louisiana, came upon hard times and could not afford to send his daughter to college. She borrowed money from an uncle to finance her education (student debt is not reserved to the 21st century). This level of education was unique in rural Louisiana in the 1920's.

She was teaching French in the high school when she met Felix at a local drug store. They were married at St. Martin's Church in St. Martinsville, Louisiana on

September 4, 1928. Felix's work took him from Louisiana to St. Louis, where they settled and raised their family.

After the rousing introduction by Mary Ann, the plans for Shirley's wedding went into high gear. My only assignment was to buy three ties for the groom, best man, and the usher. Since the three of us were wearing conservative brown suits, it seemed appropriate to buy three bright brown plaid ties. Wrong! I was sent back to get three black silk ties. Apparently, there is a Cajun book of etiquette that states that the groom must wear a black silk tie with a brown suit for a morning wedding in June.

Shirley Ann Martin, June 24th, 1961

My father, my bride, the guy she married, and Mary Ann the Great

In any event, the wedding took place on June 24th, 1961 at St. Clement's Church. The maid of honor was Mary Ann Martin, and the best man was my father. Shirley's brother, Bob Martin, was the usher. It was a beautiful sunny June day and the reception was held at Schneithorst's Restaurant. After a lovely brunch with the appropriate toasts, we returned to the Martin's home where my parents and my sister Mildred got to know my new in-laws in a pleasant and comfortable setting. From there we were off to Chicago and the Drake Hotel for a three-day honeymoon.

"For better, for worse – what did we just agree to?"

7
INTERNSHIP
AND RESIDENCY

Within a two-week period, my life had changed dramatically. On June 16, 1961, I was a single man, a student, and unemployed. On July 1, 1961, I was married, a real doctor, (or so the State of Missouri said) and had a job.

We returned to St. Louis to take up residency at 4567 Laclede Avenue in the city. The house was an apartment building owned by St. John's Hospital and used to house the interns and residents. It was part of my salary, in addition to the $125 stipend. When we arrived there, we found a drunk sleeping on the front steps. Shirley seemed a little shocked, but I assured her that he was the doorman. There was a saloon next door, and this seemed the logical place for him to sleep it off. The more discreet drunks would sleep in the basement.

The new apartment's interior décor must have been designed by one of the drunks during an especially bad hangover. The walls were pale green, and the floor was black linoleum tile with multicolored speckling. The furniture consisted of a blond desk and a chair from my room in Pittsburgh and furnishings that were stored in the basement of another apartment owned by the hospital. Immediately after moving into the second-floor apartment, Shirley had the window that opened onto the front portico nailed shut, even though it was a warm summer day with no air conditioning.

Shirley had transferred from her job in Pittsburgh back to Monsanto, so I felt that I had married into wealth. The first indication that the honeymoon was over occurred less than a week into the internship. I had been up all night on the emergency room shift from midnight to eight am Arriving home, I wanted to get some sleep and crawled into bed. Shirley, who was an early riser, was in the kitchen doing some work.

Since the layout of our three-room apartment was entry into the living room, then into the bedroom, then into the kitchen with no door separating the rooms, every move from the kitchen to the living room required going through the bedroom. As Shirley was making the trip through the bedroom, I gruffly mentioned that the sheets were wet. She replied that she had just gone to the laundromat that morning before I had come home, and that if I would be quiet and would go to sleep, the wet sheets would not bother me. At this point it became apparent that the honeymoon was over and it was time to move on with our married lives.

Shirley and Harry – a.k.a. Lucifer and St. Peter

This meant making new friends and progressing in my medical education. The choice of St. John's (now Mercy Health Care System) for the internship was multifactorial. First, I wanted to go to a hospital outside of the Pittsburgh area because of the broadening experience it would provide. Other places that impressed me were Lankenau

Hospital in Philadelphia as well as Georgetown University Hospital and hospitals in Baltimore and Cleveland. As the selection process moved along during my senior year, I became aware of how close my fiancée was to her family, so St. Louis was indeed a valuable contender.

The Christmas before our marriage, I visited the Martin family and had two hospital interviews. One was at St. Luke's Hospital and was arranged by their next-door neighbor, Dr. Frerking. The other was at St. John's. Both hospitals had a very impressive house staff. What made St. John's the favorite were some of the interns and residents that I met during the visit. Dan Martin, Phil Higgins, Alan Thiel and others were people that I would feel comfortable working with. The clincher was Mary Lou Martin showing me the new toilet that had recently been installed in their apartment. Needless to say, Shirley was elated when the matching results gave us our first choice. She did not coerce this choice in any way and, in retrospect, it turned out to be an excellent decision.

Intern orientation on June 30th listed the first assignments. My first rotation was a month's stint at the old St. Louis City Hospital. It was to begin at 12:01 am on July 1st. The doctor conducting the orientation asked if there were any questions. I raised my hand and asked the location of the city hospital and who would be the supervising physician. The answer was that the hospital was not in the best part of town, that I would be the only doctor on duty, and I would be briefed by the doctor going off duty. The orientation in the emergency room lasted all of five minutes and consisted of showing me the collection of drunks, people with lacerations, and other sundry patients waiting to be seen. He then introduced me to the police guard, wished me well, and left for greener pastures.

The intern year whizzed by in a blur of working, learning, and making new friends. Planning for specialty training became the next order of business. Primary care was excluded because of the broad field of knowledge that it entailed. Psychiatry was also dismissed, even though it was a fascinating field that had given me a most useful understanding of people and their behavior.

The Freudian school of thought at the University of Pittsburgh was a turnoff. The psychiatric faculty were very intelligent but very rigid in their approach to patient care. In many instances, they ignored fact or reality if it did not fit into their theoretical concepts.

What really interested me was a surgical field that would have a less extensive body of knowledge than some of the other specialties. Orthopedics appeared to fit this concept. So, for the first rotation of the intern year, I requested orthopedics. This service consisted of one month in the emergency room at the old St. Louis City Hospital and a month on inpatient orthopedics at St. John's.

My desire for this field rapidly waned. The first thing that became apparent was that the lifestyle of an orthopod was out of phase with an orderly daily routine. A good part of this specialty was on an emergency basis related to trauma. The clincher, however, occurred while scrubbing in on a hip prosthesis with an older practitioner. He had reached the point of placing the prosthesis into the hip socket. It would not fit, and a large hammer was ineffective. He then instructed the anesthesiologist to grasp the patient under the armpits, and the surgeon and I were to grasp the leg and pull. The first attempt did not work. So, we prepared to give a more strenuous pull. This time we gave a mighty and sudden pull. The prosthesis snapped into place, the drapes collapsed, the anesthesiologist lost his grip, and the patient slid off the table onto the floor. At this point it dawned on me that the phrase "neat and clean" did not always refer to community-based orthopedics.

The holiday season arrived and on Christmas Eve, my duty assignment was the St. John's Emergency Room. Shirley joined me in the hospital cafeteria for dinner. As we were dining, Sister Oliver joined us. She was an Irish immigrant and Sister of Mercy who stood four foot eight and spoke in an Irish brogue. If leprechauns were females, Sister Oliver would have been a perfect one. While dining, I was paged to report to the ER stat (physician lingo for 'immediately').

Sympathizing with our plight on our first Christmas Eve together, she suggested that for the celebration of the Birth of Christ, all emergencies should be sent to Jewish Hospital.

During the internship, I became intrigued with ophthalmology. It certainly was challenging surgery. Ophthalmologists Vincent Jones and Harold Bailey were often on the OR schedule and I took every opportunity to scrub in with them. In addition, a rotating type of internship presented the opportunity to see how this specialty impacted every other field of medicine. Also, physicians in this field led a more orderly lifestyle. Therefore an application was submitted to the University of Pittsburgh. An acceptance shortly followed with the stipulation that I complete my required two-year military service first.

Later that year on a Sunday afternoon, I received a phone call from Dr. Robert Mattis, the Chairman of the Department of Ophthalmology at St. Louis University. He stated that he had heard of my interest in the field and asked if I would like to come to his house and discuss this. I drove over to this huge dilapidated house and spent several hours with him.

He said he had gotten some good reports about me from the hospital staff and was prepared to offer me a position for the upcoming academic year. I asked for a tour of his facilities and to meet with current residents. This was done the following week and although the facilities were Spartan, the residents that I met were impressive. Dr. Walter Stafford was the chief resident and another close friendship developed that would last through the years. So, another fork in the road was taken. Where would this one lead? Shortly thereafter, as I was completing an application to enter the Berry Plan, I asked Shirley to make a copy of it at work. She looked at it and asked if I had not made a mistake and written ophthalmology instead of orthopedics. This is where she learned of this fork in the road.

For those people who were never subject to the military draft, the Berry Plan needs to be explained. After World War II, all males 18 years of age were required to register for the draft. While still in high school, I was classified as 1-A. To continue my education in college, it was necessary to participate in an R.O.T.C. program, so I joined the Air Force program at Georgetown. This exempted me from the draft for the first two years of college. Since I did not want an Air Force commission at this time, it was necessary to drop the program. I was immediately re-classified 1-A and put in the Washington D.C. draft pool.

The U.S. forces had just landed at Inchon, Korea (at the exact spot where we would be living in a few years). Even though General MacArthur's army was now on the offensive, the combat deaths in our forces were approaching

23,000 plus many more wounded, and the military needed warm bodies.

In February 1957, I was ordered to report for an induction physical at the D.C. draft board. A phone call to the draft board telling them I was on crutches and temporarily disabled fell on deaf ears. Arriving at the station, I was escorted to a large room for the written intelligence test. There was only one other Caucasian in this room of 100 plus draftees. After the written test, a sergeant said that he would call our names and scores. Those who scored over 15% were to proceed to the physical exam area. Most scores were in the 10-30% range. When Brady 98% was called, everyone looked around and saw a scrawny white kid on crutches making his way through the crowd to the physical exam room.

The eyes, ears, nose, and throat were checked and deemed adequate for the military. Then it was standing in line in your shorts waiting for the doctors to come back from lunch.

While standing in line, a doctor came by and saw a very visible fresh 24-inch scar running down my left leg. He asked me what in the world was I doing there. He took my chart and reclassified me 4-A on the spot and dismissed me. This provided another one-year deferment. And by that time, I was in medical school and that also gave another four-year deferment.

The residency at SLU was a marvelous experience, due in great part to the chief resident, Walter Stafford. He was an excellent teacher and academician. The others were also fine men to be associated with. The faculty had no full-time members. Dr. Robert Mattis, the chairman of the department, was one of the most bizarre personalities I have ever met outside of a locked ward. Dr. Stephen Bowen, fresh from the Mayo Clinic residency program was newly-appointed to the faculty. His brilliant mind and research interest added immeasurably to my education. Dr. Anwar Shah was also a new member of the faculty. He had just completed a fellowship at Harvard in Diseases and Surgery of the Retina.

As a first-year resident, I was placed on the retina service and for staffing reasons, remained on this service for all three years of the residency. As a result of this, in addition to my training in comprehensive ophthalmology, it provided the experience to become a competent retinal surgeon.

There is an old adage among surgeons: "You cannot learn to operate unless you operate." Well, this was a working residency and from the beginning each day included some time in the operating room. Some days it was all day and into the night. This was in the days before Medicare and the charity clinics were huge with many uninsured patients. The result was that the residents in training operated on a large number of patients. By the third year, the chief resident was a much better surgeon than a good number of the attending staff. We learned by doing.

Another doctor who contributed to my surgical training was Dr. Joe Casey. He had a large indigent practice in East St. Louis. This demographic of patients included many people with untreated major ocular pathology. He had lost the use of his left hand due to an injury. Joe would schedule his surgical cases every Wednesday morning and the chief resident would actually do the surgery for him. It would be possible to mention to him that you had not done much glaucoma surgery or corneal transplants and find that the next Wednesday's schedule included this type of surgery.

During the residency program at SLU, all residents were required to participate in some type of research project. With the guidance of Dr. Steve Bowen, a protocol was designed to study the effect of catgut sutures in corneal lacerations. Rabbits were obtained and the surgery was performed without incident. Now came the difficult part.

Have you ever tried to put drops and ointment into a mad rabbit's eyes? The rabbits did not think this was such a good idea. With the assistance of another resident, a technique was developed. My colleague would reach into the cage and grab the rabbit by the ears and sling the patient out and secure him between his knees while holding onto the ears for dear life. My job was to squirt the drops and ointment into the rabbit's eyes before he could escape. The final result was that the caretakers in the lab got to have rabbit stew at the end of the project, and the research paper was presented at the Southern Medical Society in Memphis, Tennessee.

As a final note, there was the shocking experience to see overt racism in this southern city. We stayed at the King Cotton Hotel where the restrooms were prominently designated for "Whites Only" or "Blacks Only."

Living in St. Louis offered a pleasant lifestyle with the Martin family being very supportive of the newlyweds. My salary increased from $125 to $200 a month, but we lost the rent-free apartment. This necessitated a move to Lafayette Avenue and we rented a smaller – but much nicer – apartment, including all utilities for $80 a month. We purchased a room air conditioner and were on "Easy Street."

We both wanted a family but had some setbacks at the beginning. Shirley had a miscarriage during the internship and then a second one during the first year of the residency. Adoption was being considered when a third pregnancy occurred. This time we went to Dr. J.B. Martin who specialized with the problem of recurrent miscarriages. Shirley carried this pregnancy to term and we were ecstatic with the arrival of Bill Brady in May of 1965. Our lives changed forever with the cutest and brightest child on earth.

The next move was to go to Boston to begin a fellowship in Pediatric Ophthalmology at Harvard's Boston Children's Hospital. Shirley and I had driven there earlier for an interview and funding from the N.I.H. had just been approved. However, another fork in the road suddenly appeared, and we would have no choice as to which fork to pursue.

In the early 60's, the need for military doctors became more acute, and the lack of well-trained specialists resulted in the military using inadequately-trained people in these positions.

As the result of the Tonkin Bay incident, in which the destroyer, the U.S.S. Maddox, was fired upon by the North Vietnamese, Congress responded by authorizing President Lyndon Johnson to retaliate, and he did so by bombing Hanoi.

According to the Berry Plan, if a doctor had a position in an accredited residency program, he could obtain a deferment until his specialty training was completed by accepting a commission. It seemed better to complete my training first and then go on active duty. So now we have a scrawny 2nd Lieutenant with no uniform and yet he's a commissioned officer.

After six months, the Army sent me a letter that said I was such a good soldier that they promoted me to 1st lieutenant. I still did not have a uniform and was never on an army base.

As soon as I finished my residency, the Army said I was such a good soldier, that now I was a captain and should report for active duty.

Both the Army and God act in mysterious ways.

Now, the Army did not need pediatric ophthalmologists. They needed combat surgeons. The orders advised us that dependents would be a distraction to basic training in San Antonio, but how could I leave Bill behind after we had waited so long for him to arrive?

We bought San Antonio newspapers and determined that short-term apartment rentals were available. We packed our 1960 Ford Falcon coupe to capacity with all of our earthly possessions. On a beastly hot July 3rd day in 1965, we set out on another adventure. With no air conditioning, and Shirley holding Bill on her lap with his bottle sterilizer between her feet, we made the 900-mile trek to San Antonio.

8
WE'RE IN
THE ARMY
NOW

In 1965, a newly-promoted captain reported to Fort Sam Houston for basic training amidst political assassinations, the Civil Rights Movement, and the Cold War.

Fort Sam was the basic training facility for the doctors and dentists being inducted into the Army. It also housed the Medical Field Service School that teaches the doctors how "to preserve the fighting strength." San Antonio's temperature never went below ninety degrees, even at night during July and August. Fortunately, Shirley and I were able to find a small air-conditioned apartment.

On the first day of my military life, I met an internist from Chicago, Bob Caplan. We were standing in line to pick up our uniforms and began a friendship that would last forever. We were assigned to the same squad with a classmate of mine from the University of Pittsburgh, Murray Charlson.

The Army in its infinite wisdom decided that we would be better combat surgeons if we learned how to march in close-order drill. A total fiasco ensued. The Army also felt that we would be better doctors if we crawled under rolls of barbed wire as they fired live ammunition tracers over our heads with a machine gun. The Army also believed that we would be better military doctors if we learned how to fire an M-14 rifle while walking through the woods with a bunch of other doctors on either side of you shooting at pop-up cardboard figures. This was one of the scariest things I encountered during my entire military service. It was the first and last time I have ever fired a weapon.

To become a combat surgeon, the Army allotted two hours to attain this status. It began with a one-hour lecture featuring a gruesome slide show. Then, for the second hour and in groups of three, we were assigned a goat. Instructions were to wrestle the goat down and put it to sleep with a syringe full of Nembutal. Then a sergeant came along and shot the goat in the hip with a .45. Next, we were to put the goat on a table and care for the wounded.

Now the two other doctors assigned to our goat were psychiatrists. One of them turned pale during the prior slide show and was sitting on the ground trying to retain his breakfast. The second psychiatrist informed me that he had never been in an operating room during his medical school and residency training. So, I was elected to save the goat. After about thirty minutes, the bleeding had been stopped and the wound was clean of all dead tissue and debris.

Things were looking good until the goat began to wake up and decided that wasn't a fun experience. More wrestling and more Nembutal settled that discussion. At this point, a colonel came by and inspected the wound. He then took our permanent records and officially declared all three of us as certified combat surgeons.

After six weeks, orders were issued, and my assignment was to the 121st Evacuation Hospital in Bupyeong, Korea.

121st Evacuation Hospital – Korea, 1965-66

Korea was considered a hardship tour and dependents were not authorized for this thirteen-month assignment. I learned the person I was to replace was Major Melto Goumas. I also learned that his wife and two children were there. I contacted him as to the chance of Shirley and Bill joining me and any other advice he could offer. He was a graduate of the Naval Academy and after his active duty obligation to the Navy, went to medical school. After medical school, he joined the Army completing his ophthalmology residency at Walter Reed Hospital.

In any event, he understood how the military worked, and he knew how to get things done. We worked an arrangement that, after I replaced him in Korea, I would assume the rent on the house his family was living in on the compound of a missionary radio station that broadcast into North Korea.

Shirley, Bill, and I left Fort Sam Houston and returned to her parents' home in St. Louis. After a few days, I shipped out to Seattle where I boarded a plane to the "Land of the Morning Calm." As our plane was landing, it was a bright and sunny day and the rice paddies were a brilliant green. My first impression was that this place must not be as bad as everyone says.

That notion was promptly dispelled when we stepped off the plane into 95-degree heat and 90 percent humidity and the stench from the human fertilizer used in the rice paddies permeating the air. We were billeted that night with a group of soldiers who had just come off the D.M.Z. (demilitarized zone) separating North and South Korea. They were bonkers after thirteen months of staring down 500,000 North Korean soldiers waiting for orders to invade south of the 38th parallel.

The next morning, we went to our assignment at the 121st Evacuation Hospital. Mel Goumas and I hit it off almost immediately. His experience in the military proved invaluable to a captain in his first deployment. He taught me how to play the game and advised how to have Shirley and Bill come to Korea as tourists. Mel and his family left two weeks after my arrival, and now I was the Chief of Ophthalmology (and the only ophthalmologist) for the 75,000 8th U.S. Army forces in Korea.

When Shirley and Bill arrived at Kimpo International Airport, I met them, and we drove to our new home in the commanding officer's station wagon. Our commanding officer, Col. Franklin, was likely unaware of his generosity in our use of his car and driver.

We moved into the first floor of a converted school-house. It was a brick building with running, albeit contaminated, water. There was indoor plumbing. In the kitchen, we hooked up a gas range to a propane tank. The living room was furnished with a desk and a mess hall table and several mess hall chairs. There was also a field operating room table and a cot we used as a couch. There was a small bedroom for Bill with a crib that I had bought in Seoul. The master bedroom was furnished with two beds, two dressers, and several army blankets. All of the furniture was army issue and the supply sergeant did not understand how all this furniture would fit into my 6x12 room in a Quonset hut.

Post-op ward, Capt. Hazel M., Capt. Brady, and Lieutenant Dave Gillis

My friend, Lieutenant Dave Gillis, commandeered a 2.5-ton truck and the move to our new home was complete. The compound was fenced in and there was a security guard. Our living room window overlooked the

Yellow Sea and the sunsets were magnificent. The rich colors as the visible spectrum fading into a deep purple would silhouette a sampan on the horizon and Korea at this time was as beautiful as any place on the planet. This was the exact place where General MacArthur's troops landed during the Battle of Inchon.

Over several months, other wives came to Korea as tourists and moved into houses on the compound. Our commanding officer did not like this arrangement at all, and so with our small group of friends, it became us against him. As army doctors, we did our job and provided a very high standard of care for the troops. The 8th U.S. Army saw that we were "preserving the fighting strength" so they pretty much left us alone. The fact that one of our group was treating the Adjutant Colonel for gonorrhea also helped keep the brass off our backs. Gonorrhea in the 1960's was not considered a service-related disease and would result in a black mark in the career officer's permanent medical record. Therefore, in this officer's permanent medical record, he was being treated with penicillin for sinusitis.

Military service in general, and Korea in particular, provided lessons in life that have lasted forever. One night illustrated those lessons dramatically. The first was that if you put people in a place they don't want to be and add stress and alcohol, bizarre things happen.

One evening, a cocktail party was organized on the deck of an LST (landing ship tank) in Inchon Harbor. All of the hospital staff attended. As the night wore on, a newly-arrived second lieutenant (who fashioned himself to be God's gift to women) pinched one of the nurses, Wilma, on the butt. Wilma told him that she did not appreciate that. So he repeated this five minutes later. The response was more emphatic, and he was warned not to do it again. A third pinch ensued. Now, Wilma was a farm girl who stood five feet ten and was big-boned. Her response to the third pinch was a roundhouse right that knocked said lieutenant out cold.

Since Shirley and I had a babysitter for Bill, we left the party early. Shortly after arriving home, the ER called about an eye injury and sent an ambulance to take me to the hospital. As the ambulance was heading in, we saw a commotion at a railroad crossing.

A motorcycle was overturned on the tracks, and sitting on the side of the road was my friend, Bob Daly, the hospital psychiatrist. Next to him was his Korean girlfriend in obvious pain. In the distance were the flashing lights of the local Korean Police.

The obvious move was to put his girlfriend in the front of the ambulance, put Bob and his motorcycle in the back, and take off before the police arrived.

Now, we have the ambulance speeding toward the

Army hospital being pursued by the Korean Police with their lights and sirens blaring and an international incident in the making.

About five minutes out, I told the driver to put on our emergency lights and sirens. So as we approached the guard post, the gate went up and the Military Police waved us through and promptly closed the gates, keeping the Korean Police out.

We screeched to a halt at the ER entrance and Mr. Kim, the ER tech, came running out and threw open the ambulance doors, looked in, saw the motorcycle, turned to me and said "Now what you do, Captain?"

Another teaching incident occurred one night when I was on general emergency call in the ER. About 2:00 am, an army ambulance brought in a Korean woman who had been stabbed by her GI boyfriend at a local bar. She was in shock and the stab wound appeared to involve the liver. I contacted the surgeon on call, Dave Waugh, and he rushed to the ER. Assessing the urgency, he immediately took her to the OR and asked me to scrub in with him. He did a great job, and the woman made a full recovery.

About two weeks later, we were summoned to report to the court martial of her boyfriend. This was a very interesting insight into military justice as he was stripped of rank and sentenced to Fort Leavenworth for a lengthy stay in the stockade. As I was leaving the courtroom, two

MP's (military police) stopped me and told me that the presiding colonel ordered me back into court. My offense was that I had not saluted the colonel when leaving the witness stand.

Korea in the 1960's was a third-world country with essentially no medical care for anyone. Father Gerry Murphy was a Maryknoll missionary priest who had a parish on the road to Inchon. He would come to the hospital pharmacy once a month to see if there were any expired drugs that were to be discarded. On one such visit, he told me about many of his parishioners with eye problems. The outcome of this meeting was a vision screening at his parish, and if any of his parishioners required surgery, I was able to admit them to the army hospital. Of course, the admitting diagnosis had to be in some manner related to the U.N. forces in Korea. Therefore, some of the diagnoses were U.N. crossed eyes, or U.N. action glaucoma.

One of the most bizarre incidents was smuggling into the army hospital the body of a Korean orphan who had been struck and killed by a truck.

A Norwegian pediatrician that I had become friendly with ran an orphanage in Seoul. He brought an eleven-year-old orphan girl to my clinic and it was determined that she was severely visually handicapped secondary to corneal scarring caused by a Vitamin A deficiency. This is a condition that could be helped by a corneal transplant.

Since there was not an eye bank in Korea, we assumed that we could not help this girl. A few weeks later, my friend called me and asked if the eyes of another orphan girl who was killed in a truck accident that morning could be used as a donor eye. A plan was then devised.

Riding in the front seat of his Land Rover was the orphan who needed the transplant. The donor cadaver was in a large picnic basket in the back seat. He arrived at the front gate of the hospital compound and had the Korean MP's call me. I informed them that the little girl in the front seat had leprosy and they should not go near her. They waved the pediatrician and his two passengers through the gate without incident. There was definitely prejudice against the Koreans among some of the military personnel, so I had to recruit a sympathetic OR team that would keep the whole affair quiet. We did the transplant and my friend calmly drove back through the guard post and provided a proper Christian burial for the donor.

It was truly a hardship tour, but we did our best and it was a very productive time in more ways than one. Surgically, it was a great experience enabling me to operate every day. With 75,000 US troops and all the UN forces in the country, there was a good deal of ocular trauma that needed to be treated. With the Korean population, there were a lot of untreated and rare ocular diseases that could be helped.

Our time there was also productive from the family standpoint, since Bob Brady was born ten days after Shirley had returned to St. Louis. I am still amazed to this day how she could navigate from Korea to St. Louis while 8.8 months pregnant and with Bill, an active 15-month-old toddler. There was a major U.S. airline strike, and she had to fly on four different airlines during the 35-hour trip. I didn't want Shirley to travel from Korea to Japan alone, so the three of us flew to Japan on a Korean Airlines flight.

In Tokyo, Shirley and Bill got on a Japan Airlines flight to San Francisco where she was met there by a CIA agent (who we had become friendly with in Korea) who helped her on the next leg of the trip. She rested at his place for a few hours while his wife watched Bill and then he got her on the plane to Los Angeles where she took a connecting flight to St. Louis.

We first encountered this CIA agent and his wife when he was a major in the U.S. Army. The next contact with him was when he was a civilian in Korea and had embassy plates on his car. Another time, he was a PT boat commander and he showed up at my clinic with a North Korean spy who had some shrapnel in his eye. The story was that he had picked up this person after a small skirmish on the Yellow Sea.

After Shirley safely boarded the plane in Tokyo, I had to find my way back to the base. The plan was to catch a cab to Tachikawa Air Force Base and fly back to Korea on a military plane. All of this had to be done in less than 10 hours to not raise any red flags.

The first half of the plan worked perfectly. Upon arriving at the Air Force Base, I was put on a flight to Osan Air Base outside of Seoul. But after waiting on the tarmac for an hour, the flight was cancelled due to bad weather.

I had to wait until the next afternoon to take the same flight. When approaching Korea, the flight was diverted to Kunsan, a tiny airfield on the Western coast of Korea. The pilot offered a flight back to Japan, or we could stay in Kunsan. As the only U.S ophthalmologist in Korea, I was free to travel to any military installation in the country for consultation purposes. Since I was already AWOL, I elected to stay in the right country.

I had run into a dermatologist friend, Bob Miller, while in Tokyo, and he was on the same flight, so we joined forces and went into the "control tower" at Kunsan. It was a shed about 20 by 20 feet. We woke up the airman manning the facility and asked about the next flight to Seoul. He told us, that due to the weather, nothing was flying and that the next flight would be in three days.

The next item of business was to contact my friend, Dave Gillis, at hospital headquarters and tell him my whereabouts. Dave's response was, "Where in the world in Kunsan?!" He finally found it on a map and said that because of the weather, he couldn't dispatch a chopper to get us. He also added that our Commanding Officer, Col. Franklin, was looking for and asking suspicious questions about my whereabouts.

Now we needed to find ground transportation to get back on base. The plan evolved to board a ferry in a nearby harbor and cross a bay to a railroad station where we could take a train to Seoul, then take Army transportation back to the hospital. Sounds simple. Nothing in Korea in the '60s was simple!

Bob and I took a Korean cab from Kunsan Air Base to the harbor where we found out that the ferry had sunk during the storm.

The cab driver knew of another ferry about five miles up the coast. We arrived there and boarded a boat that looked like Noah's Ark! It was crammed with pigs, goats, and chickens going to the market. We elected to stay on the deck, rather than joining the menagerie in the main cabin.

Instead of crossing the bay, the boat went out into the Yellow Sea and turned North for about 25 to 30 minutes. When it docked, the menagerie fled inland and we were left standing on the dock. Where do we go from here?

A man came wandering by with a cart, and through rudimentary Korean and charades, we were able to communicate that we wanted to go to Seoul on the 11:00 am train. He threw our suitcases on his cart, and after a

20 minute walk, we arrived at the train station, which was mobbed.

Now we needed two first-class tickets to Seoul on the 11:00 am train. The man at the ticket counter explained that they were still waiting for the 8:30 am train, and that there were no first- or second-class tickets available, but we could get third-class tickets. The train arrived shortly thereafter, and the gates opened.

The entire mob ran to board the train as we joined up with some chickens in third-class, and off to Seoul we headed. After enduring Noah's Ark, this was nothing!

However, another hitch in the plan occurred after the baggage car caught fire as the train progressed through fields of rice patties. A two-hour delay followed as the burning baggage car was detached and pushed to a siding.

Now it was lunch time and a man came by offering squid in a bucket with hot beer. This was politely declined.

We finally arrived back on base and signed in at 11:50 pm, so theoretically, I was only AWOL for one day. The next morning at breakfast, Col. Franklin came by and said he was glad that I had made it back from my "consultation visit" to Kunsan Air Base. I am still indebted to Lt. Gillis for his imaginative explanation of my absence.

I will always remember being called to the emergency room at 3:00 am on August 3rd, 1966 to get a telegram that read, "Super Pig has Super Brother." I did not get to see Bob, my son, until he was five weeks old.

Our next move was to Fort Ord, California. This time we lived on base in army housing. It was a two-story condo with a kitchen and living room downstairs and two bedrooms upstairs. It was typical garrison living and nothing exciting and lots of kids. Each day after dinner, I would play with Bill until bedtime, and then when he went upstairs it was bonding time with Bob. From early on, we tried to practice egalitarianism with our children. After Bob went to sleep, it was time to study for my boards as I hoped to complete them before leaving the military. The future was very unsettled at this time since the fellowship in Boston was no longer available.

Then one afternoon while in the clinic, I received a phone call from an ophthalmologist in St. Louis, Dr. Marvin Koenig. He had been in practice for four years and I had met him during my residency. He had just been drafted and would have to go on active duty shortly for a two-year obligation. He wanted to know if I would be interested in taking over his practice while he was gone. The offer was fifty percent of what I would gross. I did not know if that was a good offer or not, but it was much better than not having a clue about our future. So once again, a fork in the road presented itself and we immediately went house hunting.

We had lived as transients for the first six years of our married lives, and now it was time to establish some stability for our growing family. We came to St. Louis and discovered that most lending facilities did not look too favorably on someone with no guaranteed income and no credit references. We were fortunate to meet Mrs. Gertrude LaVelle, a real estate agent who was willing to work with us. She showed us a home in York Woods that was being sold by the owner who was willing to carry the loan. So, for $1,500 down and $300 a month, we were ready to move into our first real home. Shirley, Bill, and Bob flew back from California and moved into 47 York Drive. At 12:01 am, July 4, 1967, I left Fort Ord and the U.S. Army. In our old Ford Falcon Coupe, I came home.

I was very proud to have served in the military. I did my job to the best of my ability and provided the best care I could for our troops. The army was satisfied because I helped to "preserve the fighting strength." Being a young boy who grew up during World War II gave me a sense of patriotism as the Allied Armies defeated the Nazis and the Japanese in a "just war." Neither my father nor my brother served in the military. As a child, I knew that many good people never came back to their families.

Chronologically, I am a Vietnam veteran, although my service took place in Korea. My only direct contribution to that effort was caring for wounded members of the Korean Tiger Unit that were air evacuated to the 121st Evacuation Hospital from Vietnam. In a perfect world, we would not need an army. Perhaps by my volunteering (I was not drafted!), this has helped create a situation where my children were not liable to mandatory military service.

9
SETTING
DOWN ROOTS

The drive back to St. Louis took three days. It was wonderful to arrive at our own home and have Shirley, Bill, and Bob waiting for me. My first patient in private practice was the one-eyed Martin family dog, Snoopy. He had chased a rabbit into a thorn bush and had scratched the cornea in his only eye. Fortunately, he recovered with Neosporin ointment.

Dr. Koenig's practice was in the Northland Medical Building on West Florissant Avenue in Jennings, Missouri. I arrived there the next Monday morning ready for business. He had built an active surgical practice and on the first day I was able to schedule my first cataract operation in private practice. The patient, Bernard Mager, came in and said, "I can't see and want my cataract out now!" After examining him, I agreed that this was the proper thing to do. However, I was on no hospital staff and had nowhere to admit him. I left the room and called my former professor, Dr. Mattis, at St. Louis University. He said to admit the patience under his name at the university hospital and perform the surgery. It is a dictum in surgery that "good surgery begets more surgery" and in a few months, I had an active surgical practice.

Even though I was not able to pursue the fellowship in pediatric ophthalmology, Dr. Mattis appointed me as Chief of Ophthalmology at Cardinal Glennon Hospital. This included running the teaching programs for the residents. So, three half days a week, I donated my time to this endeavor and gave some thought to pursuing an academic career.

Several factors convinced me that this was not the fork in the road to follow. First, I realized that to make this a career, it would be imperative to obtain a first-class fellowship. Secondly, it would be necessary to conduct research in the field and I was not qualified to do any meaningful work in this field. Thirdly, I was married with young children and a recent event had caused me to rethink my entire future.

During my separation physical from the army in 1967, my urine tested four plus for sugar. The Army said that they would hospitalize me for a complete medical workup if I extended my military stay. Since they would not guarantee another specific discharge date, the offer was declined. After arriving back in St. Louis, an application for life insurance required a glucose tolerance test that had a top reading of 190 with the urine again at four plus. I discussed this with an internist who advised putting me on insulin. In addition, he prognosticated that it would be about ten years until vascular complications would occur. Since I was only 33 years old at the time, this would certainly curtail my future earning power. I consulted another doctor and we decided to attempt to control with diet and weight loss. After a 25-pound weight loss and a dietary regimen, the blood sugar came down to reasonable levels, the 90-100 range. My weight has remained the same ever since, and the blood sugar levels have increased only moderately in my later years. In any event, this fork in the road led to a full-time private practice that would allow a busy ophthalmic surgeon to raise and educate his children. It also provided the option of continuing to teach in the residency program on a voluntary basis.

Dr. Koenig returned after his military service and we practiced together for several years He was a very talented surgical technician but as time went on, it became apparent that we had philosophical differences in our approach to patient care. We agreed to an amicable professional separation. So once again, a fork in the road presented itself.

A new office building was being constructed at the corner of Ballas and Clayton Roads. Lou Sachs was the builder and he offered me the first choice of office space. Shirley was given the grand sum of $150 to decorate the waiting room. We went to railroad salvage and bought the furniture for the waiting room. The equipment came from Ostertag Optical, and we went deeper in debt.

The grand opening was the Tuesday morning after Labor Day in 1970. The calculations were that it would take six patients a day to break even, but what if you gave a party and no one came? For the first four months, it was a deficit operation and then in January of 1971, we made a reassuring $400 profit. It came none too soon because the family had grown since our return to St. Louis.

On January 11th, 1969, Rebecca Ann arrived in a big hurry. Upon arriving home from the office on a Saturday afternoon, Shirley said she thought that she was starting labor. We called her doctor and alerted Grandma Martin. Even before she arrived, Shirley's water broke, and the doctor had not yet returned our call. However, based on prior labors, time was of the essence.

We went to St. Louis Maternity Hospital, but Becky was getting impatient. Shirley and Becky were whisked through admitting and into the elevator heading for the maternity ward. They never got there but went directly into the delivery room from the elevator. Becky decided not to wait for the doctor and was delivered by the nurse. Perhaps this explains why, when Becky makes up her mind to do something, people need to get out of her way! When Becky came home from the hospital, Bill and Bob had made a poster with the picture of an angel and we hung it on the front door. The Brady Family was now complete.

Prior to Becky's arrival, Shirley had the bright idea that an eight- month pregnant woman and a totally inept handyman husband could save a few dollars by wallpapering the soon-to-arrive baby's room. We would do the ceiling first and then the two dormers. A total and utter catastrophe! I ended up with wallpaper paste in my armpits and no wallpaper on the ceiling. Mr. Fitzgerald, the real handyman, did a great job and was very polite not to comment on the mess he inherited.

My practice, teaching assignments, and establishing an eye clinic at the Missouri School for the Blind made for a busy professional life. However, there was always time for family life.

Wednesday afternoons were always sacred. They belonged to the children and it was up to them to plan each week's activity. As a lesson in negotiations, each child took a week to plan the program and then convince the other two to participate. This would all have to be done when I arrived home for lunch. Fishing at the Busch Wildlife Preserve, going to the zoo, or a movie were typical outings. Shirley would stay at home and get a break from the constant responsibilities of motherhood. To me, it was a great pleasure to see our children growing up, but at times it seemed they were intent on trying to drive me crazy. There were so many fun times that it would be impossible to record them all. A few incidents, however, deserve special attention. In today's language, they would be called bonding. At the time they occurred, I felt they were golden moments.

When we moved to Dunmorr Drive (see next Chapter), Bill was eligible to play Atom-1 baseball in the Kirkwood Khoury League. When we went to sign up, all of the teams were full. We were advised that if Bill wanted to play, we would have to start a new team. I was given the names of several other boys who had inquired but were not assigned to a team. We got some old baseballs and some bats and called the first practice. It was a blustery cold spring day and Bill and I arrived at the practice field. We looked around, but no one else was there. After waiting around in the cold for about ten minutes, Bill asked, "Is this all there is to our team?" I sent him out to second base and began to hit some ground balls for him to field. As we were doing this, other boys began to straggle onto the field and we had a real team!

The culmination of this was years later when Bill and I played on the same team at Busch Stadium against a team of former Cardinals, Bill hit an inside-the-park homerun, sliding headfirst into home plate.

I think he could have scored standing up.

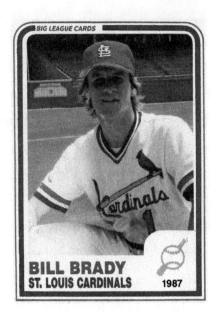

Another memorable episode occurred while we were on summer vacation floating the Colorado river. The guide said that we were in a quiet part of the river and could leave the raft and swim. Bill, Becky, and I donned life-jackets and went over the side into the river. Bob was more conservative and stayed in the raft with Shirley. Before we knew it, we were in a strong current, with Bill and Becky successfully negotiating a set of rapids. However, I was unable to get past them and ended up in a whirlpool. After swallowing half the river and nearing exhaustion, I was unable to get out of the potentially fatal current. The guide maneuvered the raft into the whirlpool where Bob was able to pull me safely back into the raft.

Bob and his 14 lb catfish

Coming home for lunch and playing catch with Becky while she wore her baseball glove like a purse or buying her a Slurpee when she was home with infectious mono were beautiful occasions. Seeing the Perfect Peanut become the Big Wheel with her red Toyota always made me feel good. She also had the first ride in the rumble seat of a Bogie, a 1934 Packard coupe. Then one day, Becky had grown up, and she and Mike got married. It was a lovely wedding and ended a segment of my life. But she will always be Perfo.

One of the big family events every year was the Christmas pageant performed by the three Brady children as Shirley was busy preparing for the holidays. The children would plan for the big production to be presented to Grandma and Grandpa Martin and Aunt Mary Ann.

Becky and Dad at father/daughter dance

Each year brought new staging and costumes. One year, it was a puppet show using old socks, one of which was black to add authenticity. Another year began with Bill introducing the Christ Child with the Johnny Carson segue, "Herrrrreee's Jesus." My favorite pageant was a movie filmed on location in Des Peres Park on a snow-covered hillside. The director had wanted to film at the zoo with camels in the background for the Magi scene. However, one of the stars threw a fit about going to the zoo in his pajamas. Actually, the three kings looked realistic with their Burger King crowns. Bob prevailed, and the production was filmed at Des Peres Park.

As the years passed, there were also sad times. On August 15, 1973, my father passed away from his second heart attack. The saddest thing to me was his unrealized potential. My mother lived in their apartment on Linden Place for another 18 years. Her brother, Bob Estel, who never married, lived upstairs and they had dinner together every night.

When Uncle Bob got out of the Army in 1946, he came to our apartment for dinner the very first day he arrived in Pittsburgh and came every night for the next 44 years!

My mother had always been a heavy smoker, so emphysema, bronchiectasis, and heart disease finally caught up with her. I remember one particular incident while she was in intensive care. Lying in bed with a tracheostomy and unable to eat or drink, she scribbled on her chalkboard that she would like a Cherry Coke. After a trip to the snack bar, I returned to her room with the Cherry Coke. She was allowed to suck on ice chips but was unable to swallow. So, with ice chips and a small sponge, she was able to have her Cherry Coke. That was the last time I saw her smile. She died on June 7th, 1991.

Finally, my brother, Charles, was a sad enigma to me. He left our family immediately after high school for the Marianist Seminary in Dayton, Ohio. I was eleven years old at the time. Through the ensuing years, I had little contact with him. He then went to Switzerland where he finished his theological studies and was ordained. He stayed in Switzerland and got his doctorate in Theology at the University of Fribourg. He returned to the University of Dayton and became head of the Theology Department.

After 25 years, he left the priesthood, married, and adopted a son. He and his wife then moved to Corpus Christi, Texas. At this point, he became somewhat estranged from the family as he divorced and lived alone. One day in 1996, while in my office, a Catholic chaplain from a hospital in Corpus Christi, Texas called me to ask if I was related to Charles Brady. I had an immediate sense of foreboding. He told me that my brother collapsed while walking through a mall. He was brought by paramedics to the emergency room but never regained consciousness before expiring.

The chaplain had reassured me that he had administered the Last Rites. There was no next of kin or people to notify in case of an emergency. The only thing they found was a very old picture of me with my office phone number on it. It remains a mystery why I was the only one in the world whose information he carried in his wallet.

10
1609
DUNMORR
DRIVE

1609 Dunmorr Drive

We moved from York Drive to 1609 Dunmorr Drive in Des Peres in July of 1972. The children went to St. Clement School and excelled in sports and academics. The front yard and driveway became our sports stadium and we played baseball, football, soccer and hockey. It did not matter which sport we played, Becky was always Joe Torre. In baseball, the boys had to make concessions to their little sister and give her ten strikes.

By the seventh grade, they had outgrown grade school and we enrolled the boys in what we considered the best secondary schools. They also excelled in these schools leading their respective classes. All three participated in soccer and this became their primary sport. Each of the children were recognized for their efforts by scholarship offers to college. They chose their own colleges and planned their own curriculum. Once again, they were quite successful in their endeavors. Shirley and I will always be proud of them and please excuse us whenever we brag. There were always some difficult times when we were rearing our family, but we always tried to do the right thing for them, even if it was difficult for all parties involved.

Some of the more memorable times at 1609 Dunmorr began in August 1974 when Frisky arrived on Bob's 8th birthday. Frisky was a barker and he always barked when Shirley turned on the microwave. His barking came to critical mass one Sunday when we returned from Mass. Frisky greeted our arrival as if he had never seen us before and Shirley had reached her boiling point. In her best Sunday outfit, a pink dress with pink high heels, she grabbed a hose and chased him back into his doghouse. Not satisfied that this was adequate discipline, she aimed the hose into the doghouse until she was vindicated.

Other notable events were related to new drivers. One morning upon rising, I found a note at the top of the staircase stating that the station wagon did not make it home that night and Bill would give details when he got up in the morning. After an immediate and rude awakening, the story was that he was slaloming down Mason Road (intentionally) in the snow and knocked a fire plug off its base. The fireplug ended up on our driveway and the station wagon returned home with bright yellow paint on the right front bumper. Bill was grounded.

Becky then decided to run an errand. She got in the station wagon and then promptly ran into the same damn fireplug again putting another streak of bright yellow paint on the left front bumper. After convincing Bill that he did not need a fireplug made into a lamp in his room, I called the water company and had them come out to recover their property.

Now Bob wanted to get into the act. So one evening, to practice his driving skills, he decided to help me by pulling a car into the garage. To get a running start, he put it into reverse and promptly backed into the gaslight on the lawn and gave us the only horizontal gaslight in the neighborhood.

Bill, Becky, Bob circa 1972

Enter Becky once again. She always wanted to outdo her brothers. One evening as I was reading in the den, she walked in and announced that the station wagon was stuck "on" the garage. We went out to the garage and fortunately, three of the four wheels were on the ground. The fourth wheel was about three feet into the air "stuck" on the doorpost. Bob and some of his friends were in the basement so they were able to lift the car down so all four wheels were safely on the ground.

Some people may think it is strange that all three of our children had mishaps with station wagons. My theory was that it may be genetic since Shirley deserved decals on one of the station wagons denoting a kill of three separate basketball stanchions. The heroes of these episodes were the three Oldsmobile station wagons that served the Brady household over a 20-year span. Each one gave us 100,000 miles of hard service.

Antique cars now entered the scene and first and foremost was 'Petunia.' She was a 1939 Packard that had seen better days. As a team, we "restored" Petunia by washing off the dirt and grime, and took her to the first and only Pond, Missouri Antique Auto Show. We went on Mother's Day because we knew that this was what Shirley wanted to do to celebrate her holiday.

As we were pulling into the parking area, we were waved over to the area where the cars were to be judged. After viewing the gorgeous cars to be judged, we were ready to head home. Just then, Shirley noticed that there were more trophies than antique cars in the judging area, so we decided to wait until all the awards were given. As we returned to Petunia, yells of excitement reigned as Petunia had indeed won a trophy.

Excitement turned to despondency the night Petunia was sold and Becky crawled under her bed and cried.

Next came 'Pierre,' a gorgeous maroon 1937 Packard club sedan. How can someone tell the gender of an automobile? My children advised me how to do this is very simple terms. "You just look at it and you can tell." I did not seek further details.

Bogie then arrived one evening at 1609 Dunmorr. Bogie

(named after Humphrey Bogart) was the most beautiful of all the antique cars. It was a 1934 Packard rumble seat coupe purchased from a museum just outside of Chicago. It was maroon and had side-mounted spare tires, white-walls and a tan leather interior. The engine was a straight eight, but it had a cracked head. I found someone in Burlington, Vermont who had the part we needed, and we performed some minor cosmetic repairs and Bogie was ready for the big time.

He was shown at the Easter Sunday Antique Car Show at Forest Park and won the best of show silver platter. He also won awards at several other car shows. Becky made it a point to be the first one to ride in the rumble seat. She also made it a point to be the first of the Brady children to sit on the new toilet seat in our upstairs bathroom.

Another old car story was when Bob and I were redoing the interior of a 1949 Packard four-door sedan. The car was a "barn find" from a farm near Lesterville. As I was pulling down the stained headliner, a few acorns fell down. The next pull on the headliner resulted in a mummified dead squirrel landing in my lap. Fortunately, all four doors of the Packard were open as I set the Olympic record for the long jump out of an antique car.

My favorite old car story is that of 'Brown Ugly.' At a local auction, I rescued a 1956 Packard that was titled to a junk yard. It was necessary to start the car with a screwdriver to drive home since it lacked an ignition. This project was to teach the children the benefits of capitalism.

At the dinner table that evening, each of them was offered a financial share of this venture. Bill stepped up first and put up some of his money. Bob contemplated the offer, and after due diligence, he added a judicious amount. Becky ran upstairs and returning with her piggy bank, emptied the contents on the kitchen table. She was all in!

Our next step was a trip to Washington, Missouri, to a man who had a field full of old-parts cars. We cannibalized hubcaps, front and rear bumpers, and an ignition from other old Packards. About three weeks later, we took the car to another antique auto auction and sold it for $450 profit. That evening, once again at the dinner table, we had a distribution of profits to a wide-eyed group of new capitalists. Shirley became involved in the delivery of the car.

A cottage at the Sugar Tree Club on the Gasconade River became a large part of the family recreational pursuits.

Tuesdays after work, Bill, Bob, and Jill joined me to go fishing. We would stop by a combination beauty parlor and live bait store on a dusty, rural road to get our night crawlers.

Very early the next morning, we would go out on the Gasconade River in a canoe. This became a great way to interact with my children in a quiet and peaceful setting.

By 9:00 am, the aroma of bacon and coffee reached out onto the river and we would dock and go up to the dining room.

By 10:30 am, it was back to the canoe for more fishing. The afternoon was spent by the swimming pool or hiking into the woods. Then by dusk, we drove home to Dunmorr Drive.

Shirley loved the peaceful setting and on weekends, she enjoyed floating the river in an inner tube or in a canoe. There were no meals to prepare, and she loved to sit on the porch and read. It was idyllic, and she called it "Our Camelot."

One summer, the club held a fishing contest. The prize was $20 for the most fish caught during the summer. Becky was 6 or 7 and entered the contest. She would go down every day when we were there and catch her favorite fish, whom she named Jimmy, and many of his Blue Gill cousins. She happily won the prize. It seemed like she caught 800,000 fish!

Another family tradition was cutting down our Christmas tree. For many years, we would go in search of the perfect tree. Rain, snow, sleet, or mud would not deter the Brady family on this quest. Even when Shirley's boots would come off in the mud, we soldiered on.

Bob would find the tallest tree in the field. To Bob's disappointment, Shirley would hold up her right arm to indicate the tallest tree we could choose. Bill would have to look at every tree in the field and then a consensus would be built. Lo and behold, every year we managed to get the perfect tree!

Grandkids Teresa and Brady Schmidt with the best Christmas tree ever

● ● ●

The 1980's were notable for the emergence of AIDS (Acquired Immune Deficiency Syndrome) on the world scene. Ronald Reagan was shot in an assassination attempt by John Hinckley. James Brady was also severely injured in the attack.

On the local scene, Chester came into our lives. He was a Yorkie and would ferociously guard the Brady household. One snowy evening, he chased a 2.5-ton fire-breathing dragon from coming into our yard. The city snowplow with its blades sparking off the concrete street and making a loud grating sound as it passed by was chased all along the perimeter of our yard until Chester felt it had been vanquished.

Then along came Daiquiri. Becky and her roommate Chris had rescued a forlorn puppy they had found at a barbecue party at Spring Hill College. They hid her in their dorm room until graduation. Since Chris and Becky each owned 50 percent of the dog, I do not know how 1609 Dunmorr ended up with 100 percent of Daiquiri. However, Daiquiri and Chester became the best of friends.

All three children attended college. Bill went to the University of California at San Diego. Since our firstborn was all alone as a freshman in a strange city, we needed to visit and take him off campus for a good meal. Since Shirley and I had never been to San Diego before, we asked Bill if there was a nice local restaurant where we could dine. He thought we might like some seafood, so he took us fifty miles into Mexico to Gaspar Ortega's Restaurant in Rosarito where we dined on lobster and drank Corona beer. The price for this meal was $8.99 per person and the view overlooked the Pacific Ocean. So much for the lonely freshman and our worries about his getting along in the world.

Another assurance that our firstborn was on his way in the world occurred when Bill called us one evening from

San Diego to tell us that he would be appearing the next morning on ABC's *Good Morning America* as a medical technician. Our children never cease to amaze us.

Our second child, Bob, went to Notre Dame. On a Saturday afternoon while watching Notre Dame's football team defeat Michigan in Ann Arbor, the camera showed some exuberant students jumping up and down in the end zone. Among 101,000 fans, there was Bob Brady in the front row.

Another college story entailed Bob leaving St. Louis in a blizzard to drive back to South Bend. He said not to worry since the Buick Riviera was a front-wheel drive and good in snowy conditions. We worried all day until he called and said that he had arrived safely. Our children never cease to amaze us.

Our daughter went off to Spring Hill College where she found out that southern belles did not play soccer because they might get their chiffon dresses muddy. She organized the first female soccer team and she became president of the Tri Delta Sorority. Next on her agenda was to threaten the national sorority over a pricing dispute that she would be selling the sorority pins at the local pawn shop. In addition to harboring a fugitive dog in her room, she managed to show up heavily beaded on Bourbon Street in New Orleans at the Mardi Gras Parade. Our children never cease to amaze us.

So, by 1988, we were empty nesters and entered the next phase of our lives. Smash tennis league continued and since Shirley and I were such versatile athletes, golf entered the picture. Westborough Country Club became the primary venue where Shirley and Harry distinguished themselves after a long, painful process. The process began with golf school in Florida. Shirley was dumbfounded on day one when her instructor pontificated on reading the green by the way the grass tilted as the day goes on. My takeaway from day one was to swing as hard as I could just in case I hit the ball.

Progress was slow but sure. Shirley astounded herself and her brother Bob by scoring a hole-in-one. I challenged the ladies' champion at Bellerive Country Club to play in the world's first (and only) unisex golf tournament. If men and women were equal in everything, why did they have men's and women's tees on golf courses? This bitter match at Miami Lakes Golf Course ended with Mrs. Phillips pitching in from 50 yards off the green to win by one stroke. However, she lost that evening to me in the smallest fanny contest with Bob Hannegam acting as the judge.

As time went on, the golfing improved. I caught up with Shirley with a hole-in-one at Westborough. As a team, Shirley and I won the Mr. and Mrs. Tournament at Westborough four years running. I was also able to win the gold medal three different times in the St. Louis Senior

Olympics golf tournaments at Forest Park.

Our children continued to shine as they pursued their careers. Bill graduated from the University of California at San Diego and entered Tufts Medical School. Bob graduated from Notre Dame and wanted a trial of research. He worked with Dr. Jay Pepose at Washington University and co-authored an article on retinal diseases in mice. Becky returned to 1609 Dunmorr and entered graduate school at St. Louis University and earned a double masters in hospital and business administration. So much for the empty nest.

Shirley and Harry at a jungle village in Haiti

Our next adventure was in Haiti. Bob, Shirley, and I flew to Cap Haitien with Captain Smedley. The plane was a single engine survivor from the 1930's. Shirley was concerned that if the plane went down in the ocean, we'd have to crawl through the door and turn left onto the wing so we didn't get hit by the propeller. The plane did have to land and refuel on the island of Georgetown Exuma. As we were coming in on our approach, there was some turbulence and Captain Smedley calmly pointed out a drug smuggler's plane on the bottom of the ocean that crashed about 25 yards short of the runway. After refueling, we did make it to Cap Haitien Airport and after the goats and chickens were chased from the runway, we made a safe landing.

Customs at the airport was a picnic table where a menacing-looking officer packing a .45 awaited us. It rapidly became apparent that he needed some encouragement to clear us and our baggage to enter his country. Since we had a suitcase full of used glasses, I pulled out a pair of Foster Grant sunglasses and advised him that since he had such an important job and was outdoors all day, he needed protection for his eyes. We immediately were cleared from customs and met our driver from the mission hospital.

One of the most gratifying experiences of my surgical career happened in Haiti. My son, Bob, had become an adept surgical assistant and had accompanied us on this trip. After a two-week stay, we were preparing to leave Haiti the next morning and most of the remaining equipment had been packed and everything else at the mission hospital had closed down.

Just then, a truck pulled into the compound and three obviously blind Haitians were led into the hospital. The story was that they had heard of the mission in their village but were unable to get someone to drive until that morning. Bob and I exchanged glances and knew that if we did not operate then and there, these patients might never get another opportunity to see again. Bob said he would unpack and get the OR ready while I prepared the patients for surgery.

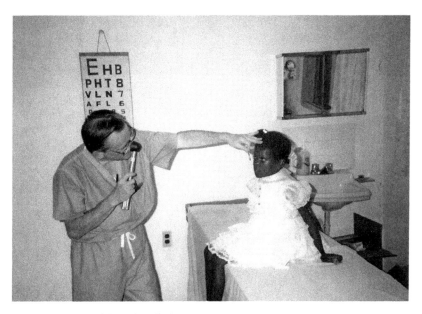

Young Haitian girl in the clinic

We did it! No ancillary personnel, no back up, no pre-op meds. Just the two of us! The next morning, we got up early, checked the patients' post-op status and sent them back in to the mountains with their eye drops. It was wonderful experience to share with my son.

Our son Bob with Michael our interpreter

11

IT ISN'T
WORK

IF YOU LOVE WHAT YOU ARE DOING

Along the way in my 56 years as an ophthalmologist, medicine has changed in many ways. However, many things have remained the same and this can be said of our society in general.

In the 1960's, Marilyn Monroe died from an overdose of a barbiturate, a prescription drug. In 2009, Michael Jackson died from an overdose of a mixture of prescription drugs. In the mid-60's, the political argument was the passage of the Medicare Law. In 2018, it has been about immigration and the battle over repealing and replacing Obamacare.

Many technological advancements of today in ophthalmology would have been mind-boggling in the 60's. In those days, there were no lasers. Contact lenses were considered a torture from the Middle Ages. Cataract patients were kept in the hospital for a week with sand-bags by their heads to prevent movement. There were large charity clinics and many people were excluded from mainstream medicine.

Today, we laser people so no one needs to wear glasses. Cataract patients are allowed to play golf on the first day after surgery. Contact lenses are so comfortable that patients can wear them weeks at a time. What has not changed is that no matter how wonderful this technology is, it does not help the patients if they are unable to gain access to the doctor or unable to afford quality care.

Over this period of time, my career in ophthalmology has exceeded by light years all of my expectations. The best answer I can give is that it has been a privilege to be a doctor. I don't know how it happened this way, but it did. It gave the scrawny little kid with the thick glasses and no real role model a sense of self-esteem.

To have patients trust me to do what is right to care for their precious eyesight is heady stuff. To be able to compete successfully with the top doctors in my chosen field is something that can never be taken away. To have the opportunity to lecture locally, nationally, and interna-tionally are opportunities that I never would have imag-ined in my formative years.

The wonderful feeling to be able to care for the homeless, to work and teach in third-world countries, these were things that the young boy sitting on the front steps of 618 Lockhart Street would never have even dreamed of.

At this point in the narrative, let me digress to some of the high points along the way. The first episode occurred while I was still in my residency training. Dr. Mattis, the Chairman of the Department of Ophthalmology at St. Louis University, was involved in a research project studying a new method for removing cataracts. He was going to a conference at Harvard and wanted to demonstrate the advantages of this new technique. To do this, he wanted to present a movie of the actual surgery (this was long before video came into vogue). He asked me to do the surgery to be filmed. So, the scrawny little kid with the thick glasses demonstrated a new surgical technique to the ophthalmology department of Harvard!

Another adventure began six weeks after the completion of the residency program. Upon arriving in Korea, I realized that I was the only ophthalmologist for the 90,000 US and UN troops in the country. Chapter 8 related the story of the Korean orphan who required a corneal transplant. Here is another war story.

Early one morning, an urgent call came from the 8th Army headquarters that General Rich, the commanding general, had a serious eye problem and was coming by Med-Evac helicopter to our hospital. My corpsman, Oscar

Delgado, took an ambulance to the helipad to await the general's arrival. I jumped out of the sack and rushed to the Red Cross Donut Dollies for a donut and a cup of coffee and proceeded to the eye clinic. Shortly thereafter, the entourage entered the clinic area. Delgado saluted me and I saluted Delgado. Then General Rich's aide, Captain Brady, saluted the other Captain Brady. Then we all saluted General Rich. Captain Brady handed Captain Brady the general's health report.

Now for the serious eye problem. The general, upon arriving that morning, said he had scratchy feelings in his left eye. After a seven-second examination, I asked Delgado for a small forceps and proceeded to remove an eyelash that had turned in and was touching the general's cornea. The general felt immediate relief. He got up and the entourage left for the waiting Med-Evac helicopter and he flew off into the heavens. The entire event took less than ten minutes. That is not the end of the story, though.

Later that day, our commanding officer, Colonel Franklin, arrived at the officer's club and proceeded to send me a drink from his usual seat at the bar. Immediately, I thought that something was wrong. He then came over and patted me on the back. Now I was sure something was wrong! However, to my surprise, he congratulated me because General Rich had cited how our hospital had efficiently "preserved the fighting strength" of the 8th U.S. Army.

After military service came private practice.

One thing that has provided a sense of a job well done is that in my 57 years in medicine, I have never been sued for malpractice. At times there were unsatisfactory results, but in these instances, honesty with the patient and assurances that I would stand by them in difficult times, was comforting to them.

This brings us to the legal profession and its adversarial nature. Testifying for both the plaintiff and the defendant gave me a good perspective on the judicial system.

First, the plaintiff: a young man was put on a drug (Plaquenil) for a determatological condition. This drug can be toxic to the retina in a small percentage of cases. The prescribing doctor was a Professor of Dermatology at Harvard. Unfortunately, the young man became legally blind secondary to the medication.

The attorney for the plaintiff contacted me to appear as an expert witness in the case. The case was settled out of court for the plaintiff.

Now for testifying for the defense: a young wife shot her husband in the face with a .357 magnum. She was on trial for first-degree homicide, being accused of shooting him while he was asleep. Her defense attorney wanted to plead down to involuntary manslaughter. He hoped to do this by proving the husband was awake and that this was a crime of passion and not premeditated. The forensic evidence showed gunpowder residue on his sclera and, therefore, the husband was indeed awake with his eyes open when the shot was fired. After my testimony, the attorney assured me this would help his client. He then made the mistake of putting the wife on the witness stand. When asked to describe the incident, she testified that, "I went out of the bedroom and got his gun and shot the rotten S.O.B. right in his mouth." So much for the expert witness and involuntary manslaughter.

Another positive feeling was to be on the teaching faculty in the department of ophthalmology at St. Louis University. Fifty-plus years of interacting with the residents in training provided me with the opportunity to meet and interact with people from around the world. This included individuals from China, Japan, Egypt, Iran, South Africa, Australia, Indonesia, Afghanistan, Nigeria, India (all three dialects), Pakistan, Bangladesh, Greece, Cuba, and Mexico.

Ophthalmologists are supposed to be involved with microscopic surgery and precision in all their duties. This assumption is proven incorrect by the following incident. A young starlet who was to appear in a movie with Tim Conway and Don Knotts was advised that she needed green eyes for the film. So, we provided that service. On a follow-up visit prior to the filming, she was in the examining chair and was instructed to remove the contacts so that her cornea could be checked for any irritation.

To demonstrate her facility with handling the lenses, she went to remove one and it popped straight up and landed in the middle of a very impressive cleavage. We looked at each other in frozen silence for a second or two. Then I judiciously left the room and sent in one of the female technicians to help recover the lost lens.

Here's a story that shows that ophthalmologists really are medical doctors first, and then become specialists. One evening at Westborough Country Club, a gentleman at our table began to choke on a piece of meat. The Heimlich procedure was unsuccessful on three vigorous attempts to dislodge the obstruction.

The diner fell from his chair, turned blue, stopped breathing, and his pupils became dilated. Realizing we had less than two minutes to act before brain death, Dan Rolfe, the assistant manager, secured for me a steak knife and called 911.

I was able to open the trachea in 30 seconds, and using the hollow portion of a fountain pen, established an airway. The diner immediately resumed breathing and the airway was maintained until the paramedics arrived and stabilized the patient for transport to a hospital.

After washing my hands to remove the blood, I noticed

that there was not a drop of blood on my white sweater.

After seeing people going blind from treatable diseases in third-world countries, several incidents convinced me that people in our St. Louis community were indeed going blind from readily-treatable disease. The primary reason was that our medical system considers them as non-persons. The homeless have no permanent address, no insurance, Medicare, or Medicaid and no money. This adds up to no treatment.

These circumstances led in 1998 to the opening of the Brady Clinic for the Homeless at the St. Louis University Eye Institute. The very first patient claimed to be hit in the eye by a "bolt of lightning" and went blind immediately in that eye. Further history revealed that she had been stabbed in that eye during a fight.

11,000 patient visits later in 2018, we are still hearing unbelievable stories when caring for the less fortunate.

Another patient's story further exemplifies the patient demographics of the clinic. A social worker from St. Patrick's Center referred a woman who arrived there one morning with a red painful eye. The history was that she was a heroin addict, drank a fifth of vodka a day, and supported her habits with prostitution (we are non-judgmental at our clinic). The red painful eye was due to a type of glaucoma that can cause blindness in a very short period of time. Immediate laser treatment was advised.

However, the patient was so agitated that she could not sit still for the laser treatment. She was admitted to the hospital, sedated and proper treatment to both eyes was accomplished.

The financial needs of the clinic are provided by the Mildred Brady and Rena Martin Charitable Eye Foundation, a 501(c)(3) not-for-profit foundation. Both grandmothers would be proud to know that the officers of this foundation are Bill Brady, Bob Brady and Rebecca Schmidt.

At this point, let me discuss why I chose medicine in general and ophthalmology, in particular, as my profession. Was it for the money? No, even though it provided a comfortable lifestyle for our family. If financial gain was my primary motivation, I could have made much, much more by exploiting my patients financially. Believe me, some of my colleagues have followed that road.

As referenced in Chapter 1, at the age of three days, I was baptized into the Catholic Church. As my life progressed, I received the Sacraments of Holy Eucharist, Reconciliation, Confirmation. I became an altar boy, attended Catholic grade school, high school and college. I studied the Scriptures and was impressed by the parable of the talents. God has blessed me with a certain set of talents and my duty was to utilize them to the best of my abilities.

12
THE
HOME

Tuesday, October 12, 2015, was a sunny fall day when another fork in the road occurred. On this date, Barack Obama was the president of the United States and the Democratic Party would eventually nominate Hillary Clinton to be his anointed successor the following summer. In the Republican party, a billionaire reality show host had announced that he would seek the nomination to run against her.

In more mundane circumstances, Shirley and I made the move to Friendship Village, Sunset Hills, a retirement community. After 43 years at 1609 Dunmorr, this was a major project. With the help of Sunset Move Managers, this was accomplished in only one day. Since our home was sold as a cash deal, in "as is" condition and with no contingencies, we moved earlier than planned into a rental villa while our new villa was being completed. We informed our friends that our children had "stuck us in the home."

Stuck in the Home

As our new villa was being built, we were able to monitor the construction. It would be a 1460-square foot living area with a full basement. Becky insisted on a basement because of the tornado risk in Sunset Hills. As the new villa was being built, it became apparent that the door to the basement patio was being put in the wrong place. To go outside from the basement to the patio, we would have to crawl through a window! Only after the threat of withholding payment did the construction company finally admit that they had made a mistake and put the door in the right place. Our final move into the new villa was on March 23, 2016. Shirley's choices of the carpeting, painting, décor, and furnishings were outstanding.

Meeting new friends and assimilating into the community went very smoothly. Shirley would continue going to Daily Mass at St. Catherine's Church, a five-minute drive from our villa. I joined a men's group each morning for a continental breakfast. This group included a chicken farmer from Iowa, an engineer from Monsanto, the president of Maritz Travel Company, an ophthalmic surgeon, a heavy construction equipment operator and several others.

Some of the more interesting people I met were older veterans who served in World War II: a man who landed on Omaha Beach on D-Day, another who was with General Patton's armored division in the Battle of the Bulge. A third man was with the O.S.S. (the precursor of the CIA.) and was placed in China behind the Japanese lines to organize a guerilla force. All had amazing stories to tell.

We have made some observations on life at the Home while sitting in the last pew at Mass. From this vantage point, the congregation looks like a box of Q-tips in God's waiting room. After Mass, it is necessary to leave promptly, or risk being run down by speeding electronic scooters.

Shirley has continued serving as a Eucharistic minister at St. John's Mercy Hospital on Sundays and is also volunteering in the skilled nursing unit here at Friendship Village. I have been asked to work on developing an endowment fund for those elderly residents who are running out of money. Some people have been residents here for 40 years. Inflation has eaten up their assets and fixed-dollar pensions cannot cover their needs. We need to assure that these residents can remain here in dignity for the rest of their lives.

Dinner and/or lunch are covered in our monthly fee, so Shirley is thrilled at not having to cook. All of our outdoor and indoor maintenance is also included, so we are really living on Easy Street at this point in our lives.

Grandson Donovan Brady ready to hit

Grandson Griffin Brady and his 12 lb sea bass

Retirement is a time to watch grandchildren grow and flourish. Griffin, our oldest grandchild, has graduated from the University of Pittsburgh and is contemplating his next career move. Donovan is a freshman at Drexel University and leans towards a scientific career. Teresa is a junior at Cor Jesu Academy and has become a field hockey star, scoring the winning goal for the league championship. Brady, another grandchild, almost singlehandedly led St. Gerard's to the CYC baseball championship, throwing out three potential base stealers and collecting two hits. I recently learned that he was awarded a four-year scholarship to DeSmet Jesuit High School. Lastly, we have Morrie, who makes friends wherever he goes with his smile and pleasant personality. He is my special pal.

Poppy and his pal Morrie

The Schmidt family, Teresa, Becky, Mike, and Brady

Cousins Donovan Brady, Griffin Brady, and Teresa Schmidt.
"Who's in charge?"

I cannot leave the topic of grandchildren without mentioning this pearl of the Brady DNA. Teresa managed to back her car, Pickle, into a fireplug, joining Bill, Bob, and Becky in their early driving exploits. The question here is, is the Martin DNA also active in these mishaps?

While trying to be retired, I found that more forks in the road presented themselves.

Channel 5 and Mike Bush produced a video featuring the Brady Clinic, which was aired on his *Making a Difference* segment. The filming took place at the St. Louis University Eye Institute, and it lasted for two and a half hours. This was edited down to a three-minute on-air segment. Apparently, Mike and Channel 5 thought it was a very good piece because they aired it on five different days over a two-month period of time. Mike is a pro. He was extremely easy to work with, and it was a gratifying experience for me.

Palm Desert 1998 with Bob Brady and Don Miller

EPILOGUE

So, this brings us back to the blizzard on St. Patrick's Day 2000 and wondering, "How did it all turn out this way?" The scrawny old guy wearing glasses does not know. Part of the answer likely has to do with two remarkable women. The first is Mildred Brady, my mother. When we did not have money to buy potatoes, she would cut up bread crusts and brown them in grease and call them "potato substitutes." Then she would reassure me that "we will manage" and we did!

My Mother – Easter 1991

The second remarkable woman was a very sophisticated young lady from St. Louis who came into my life, Shirley Ann Martin. She helped me choose the proper forks in the road. As it says in the song, "She is my hero; she is the wind beneath my wings."

Shirley is a remarkable person who always strives to do the right thing. She devoted her life to her children by being the best mother she could be. When self-doubts and agnostic thoughts would trouble me, she was always there and would lead by example. She always did it with a good sense of humor. At one of my more bizarre events, the movie *Whatever Happened to Rick and Ilsa,* she wore a sweatshirt that read "My next husband will be normal."

So now our children are grown and have their own wonderful families. The life cycle is repeating with Griffin, Donovan, Teresa, Brady, and Morrie.

How do I answer the question of my very being and having such a wonderful life? Is there Divine Providence and a loving God or is all the universe just the result of a spontaneous high thermodensity explosion?

The late Stephen Hawking, the most brilliant astrophysicist of our era, says in his book, *The Grand Design,* "The laws of nature tell us how the universe behaves, but they don't answer why. Why is there something rather than nothing? Why do we exist? Why this particular set of physical laws and not some other?" He further states that it is reasonable to ask who or what created the universe and if some entity exists that needs no creator, that entity is God.[1]

As first described in 1924 by the Belgian priest, Georges Lemaitre, our expanding universe can be traced back to a single point in time, the Big Bang. Can these two concepts be united in a single explanation of our universe as we know it today?

Time began for our planet, Earth, at the instant that the explosive energy of the Big Bang condensed, resulting in the formation of matter. We only know what happened after time began. Space and nothingness (eternity?) preceded this. Could the spontaneous energy of the Big Bang be the "God Particle" that the astrophysicists of today are seeking?

If so, then these two philosophical concepts of the existence of God and the Big Bang can come together in a unified theory that has resolved my agnosticism of 64 years. For all recorded time, mankind has sought after a Supreme Being, and now through the lens of Faith, Hope, and Scientific Reason, I am confident in the answer.

Let me finish with a quote from William Shakespeare's *As You Like It*. "All the world is a stage and all the men and women players. They have their entrances and exits and one man in his time plays many parts...then there comes

---

1   *The Higgs Boson: Searching for the God Particle.* Scientific American, 2012.

the last scene of all that ends this strange eventful history."

"What did we agree to Jun 24, 1961?"

Acknowledgements

At the end of any successful project it is a pleasure to thank those who offered critical help.

First of all, to my editor, Ellen Gable Hrkach, past president of the Catholic Writers Guild. Ellen's timely and effective critique put my thoughts into a much more cohesive narrative.

To Cathy Gilmore, whose comprehensive knowledge of faith-based writing added substance and gravitas to the project. I look forward to the ongoing success of her newest concept, VirtueWorksMedia.com

To Trese Gloriod, for a spectacular cover design and layout expertise.

To Joseph Silver, whose soft spoken suggestions added to the religious aspects of the book.

To Zip Rzeppa, without your enthusiasm, encouragement, and spiritual drive, this project would never have come to fruition.

And lastly to my wife, Shirley, and the flying pig that got off the ground.

ABOUT THE AUTHOR

Harry R. Brady is a retired ophthalmic surgeon and clinical Professor of Ophthalmology at St. Louis University. He and his wife, Shirley, live in the wonderful retirement community of Friendship Village Sunset Hills in suburban St. Louis.